Song of the Open Road:
An Autobiography and Other Writings

Song of the Open Road:
An Autobiography and Other Writings

by Paul Weston and Jo Stafford

Foreword by Tim and Amy Weston
Edited by Keith Pawlak

BearManor Media
2012

Song of the Open Road: An Autobiography and Other Writings
by Paul Weston and Jo Stafford
Edited by Keith Pawlak

© 2012 The Weston Family Trust

All rights reserved.

No part of this book may be reproduced without written permission, except for brief quotations embodied in literary articles or reviews.

For information, address:

BearManor Media
P. O. Box 71426
Albany, GA 31708

bearmanormedia.com

Photographs courtesy of the Paul Weston and Jo Stafford Collection at the University of Arizona School of Music

Typesetting and layout by John Teehan

Published in the USA by BearManor Media

ISBN—1-59393-287-1
978-1-59393-287-9

Contents

Foreword · vii

SONG OF THE OPEN ROAD

Introduction · 1

THE BEGINNINGS
Paul Weston · 5
Jo Stafford · 11

THE DAYS OF THE BIG BANDS
Introduction · 21
Road Managers · 23
The High and Low Roads of Bobby Burns · 27

THE DORSEY YEARS
The Battle of the Dorseys · 35
The Song of the Open Road · 37
Frank Sinatra · 47
An Embarrassing Moment · 49
The Leader · 51

THE BUSINESS OF MUSIC
Tin Pan Alley · 59
Jerome Kern · 63
The Capitol Records Story · 65
Jonathan and Darlene Edwards · 71
The Ducks Are Drowning! · 79

CORRESPONDENCE · 87

ESSAYS BY PAUL WESTON
Roy Harris, Record Labels, and Musical Progress   155
The Hit Psychology   159
What *Is* Bop?   165

Editor's Notes   169

Acknowledgements   173

APPENDIXES
Ballplayers and Players   177
Chapter Outline   179
Correspondence, Jo Stafford and Johnny Mercer   187
Singing Star Stafford by Jehanne Warrington   189

Bibliography   193

Notes   195

Index   203

Foreword
by Tim and Amy Weston

A FEW YEARS AGO I was having dinner with some old grade school friends. After all these years we still stay in touch and get together once in a while. At one point the conversation turned to talking about our parents at which point one of my friends said, "You know Tim, we had no idea how famous your Mom was!" Reflexively I immediately replied, "Neither did I!" This was not meant to be a glib or funny reply. Growing up in my family, that's exactly how things were.

I think that this was the result of the fact that though our parents took their creative work seriously, they didn't take themselves seriously. There wasn't any pretense. My sister and I weren't growing up as the children of Paul Weston and Jo Stafford. We were never made to feel that way. It was us and Mom and Dad.

Occasionally during our childhood, particularly as we were becoming teenagers and feeling our independence (or imagining it) our Dad felt that we didn't appreciate our mother's notoriety. He would sometimes out of the blue grace us with the following statement, "You know you kids have NO idea how famous your mother was." For Amy and I there was no good response to this other than admitting that due to their modesty regarding their musical careers, we really didn't have any idea.

Granted, not everyone's Mom could be seen on TV or heard on the radio, or had their latest recordings debut at home before anyone else heard them, but this was all in the context of a larger incredibly normal and stable upbringing. By the time my sister and I were of age, Dad went to work all week long at CBS or NBC and Mom was for all intents and purposes a stay-at-home Mom who usually slept in until 11am. She was always a night owl.

Don't get me wrong. There were housekeepers, gardeners, laundry ladies, two Cadillacs and a house in Beverly Hills with a swimming pool and room for two ponies (I made up that last bit about the ponies), but this doesn't describe the quality of parenting I believe we enjoyed or the nuclear family that we actually were.

Probably the only "down side" to this existence was growing up under the illusion that The Music Business was a very easy and welcoming place to have and enjoy a thriving career. That's another story and not nearly as interesting as the Weston and Stafford story.

Many years ago, my parents made an attempt at securing a book deal to write about their experiences in the music business. This was during the time when many "tell all" books were all the rage. Kitty Kelley's book on Frank Sinatra would be the poster child for this genre. Most of the publishers my parents solicited wanted *exactly* this sort of writing from them and they simply were not up for it. They refused to "dish" and, as a result, never secured a book deal. In keeping with their lack of pretense, they (particularly my Mom, the reluctant "star") were never too shook up about the absence of a book in their treasure of accomplishments.

The closest thing in this compilation to anything revealing will be to read the private letters my Mom and Dad exchanged during a very brief period of their courtship at a time when they were working on opposite Coasts. I use the word "revealing" not to comment on the subject matter of the letters, but to address the fact that these letters were never intended to be read by anyone other than the two of them. They are a charming insight into our parents' personalities, the tone of the times, and to their contributions to the music business during one of its most dynamic periods.

– Tim Weston

WHEN MY MOM passed away, my brother and I went about the task of going through everything in preparation of selling their home and all that happens when your last parent passes away. I came across this big stack of letters. Some were from my Mom to my Dad and some from my Dad to my Mom. Mom was in New York and Dad was in California during a time when they were "dating," but separated. I remember my Mom telling me that Dad would call her up and play "Laura" (their "song") for her on the piano. I knew they were very much in love, but sitting down and reading through all of these letters really made me realize (through much laughter and tears) just how much my Mom and Dad really loved, liked, and respected each other.

Growing up, we knew NEVER to try to "play" one parent against the other. They were a united front in all decisions. Once I poured through all these letters, I saw how romantic their love for each other was and grew to appreciate even more what a GREAT sense of humor they both had. We grew up with a LOT of laughter in our household and these letters and their stories truly highlight that sense of humor we all shared. I also loved reading through the letters and enjoying the historic references of the times. Mom's various gigs, differences with colleagues and all of the people they dealt with during that time. It's a beautiful love story, while at the same time being a history lesson of that period of time—through my Mom and Dad's very funny points of view.

Their stories of life on the road and their careers are SO priceless and funny. I'm very excited to share them all with everyone. I know they had trouble publishing their autobiography early on because publishers said that there wasn't enough "drama or smut." My parents were a couple that worked together. They enjoyed their years together on the road, in the studio, and performing by seeing the humor in it all—all along the way. That's how we were brought up, not that life was without its "drama" (I created most of that as a teenager), but we always learned that a sense of humor was the most important tool in all of life.

– Amy Weston

Song of the Open Road

Introduction

SONG OF THE OPEN ROAD: *An Autobiography and Other Writings* is a three-part collection of the writings of Paul Weston and Jo Stafford. The first part, an autobiography written in 1979 with the help of their friend and colleague Fred Heider, highlights the couple's beginnings and early days in the music business. The autobiography has been edited from surviving manuscripts into the current published work. Following is a series of letters written between March and September of 1945 that detail the couple's early courtship and rise into stardom. Last are three essays written by Paul Weston while he worked as the music director for Capitol Records during the late 1940s.

Supplementing the text is a number of supporting documents that are appended to add greater context to the collection. The first two appendixes relate directly to the autobiography. The first of these is "Ballplayers and Players," which is part of an unfinished chapter relating to the couple's love of baseball. Next is a draft-notated outline that was intended to be the basis for their finished book. Following are two works that directly relate to the letters. The first of these is a formal exchange between Johnny Mercer and Jo Stafford, which was written during the time of the Paul Weston and Jo Stafford letters. Last is a publicity piece regarding Jo Stafford's engagement at the La Martinique that appeared in *Band Leaders* magazine during the summer of 1945.

This collection adds to a field of literature on American music that, up until now, has said very little about the lives of Paul Weston and Jo Stafford. There are glimpses of their importance in some scattered biographies, oral histories, and in books about the swing era—but there is nothing of any length. What this text shows is that their contribution to American culture was anything but trivial. It is at times a read that is humorous, complex, and insightful. But more importantly, it is a telling of their own story in their own words.

– Keith Pawlak

The Beginnings

Paul Weston

It's not unusual for people in the entertainment business to begin their books with compelling, heart-tugging tales of dire need or spine-tingling accounts of being put upon as adolescents, but there is absolutely nothing traumatic or dramatic to report concerning our early years. Jo was born in Coalinga, California with strong evidence of Tennessee blood running through her veins. I grew up in the Berkshires of Pittsfield, Massachusetts. Our childhoods were normal, average, unprivileged, but certainly comfortable.

We've always felt that most people in show business make their mark on the strength of chance, on being lucky enough to be in the right place at the right time. Talent certainly helps, but luck is an extremely important factor that both of our careers certainly bore out.

During a calm Ivy League education at Dartmouth College I did what every young man was supposed to do those days in New England. My liberal arts curriculum involved an economics major. While I managed to end up with a *Cum Laude* honor and a *Phi Beta Kappa* key, I most assuredly had no compatibility with economics. I hated the subject. Before final exams I would re-read the entire course, outline it and then memorize the outline. This enabled me to kick the hell out of the tests and the professor who, in spite of himself, reluctantly had to give me a good grade. The only problem was what happened right after the exam.

Years later I found a comparison in a description of what can happen after a revival meeting. "You get all charged up with that old-time religion, you walk out of the hall, the cold rain hits you in the face—and everything's gone!" That's the way it was with my formal education in economics—the day after exams everything was gone.

In my innocence I went down to New York to do whatever a newly born economist does. There was somewhat of a problem. The year was

1933, the depression was in full bloom, and economists were leaping out of buildings with alarming regularity. I felt I was too young to die, particularly as an economist. So I prevailed on my parents to stake me to graduate work at Columbia University, where at least I'd be on the scene if my calling came back into favor. Having a band at Dartmouth I soon made contact with the Columbia Orchestra—The Blue Lions, and became their piano player.

In the summer following my graduation from Dartmouth I had taken my band to Missouri and there—here we go again with chance and luck—had met the mother of the pianist in the Joe Haymes band. Anyone familiar with music in the thirties knew about Joe Haymes and His Orchestra. They played at Roseland Ballroom and the McAlpin Hotel, and later became the nucleus of the Tommy Dorsey Orchestra when the Dorsey brothers decided to go their separate ways.

So I subwayed down to Roseland, looked up the Haymes piano player, introduced myself and asked how one could become a big band arranger. He gave me some advice that really changed my life, the same advice I gave to many young men who later asked me how to get started:

> If you want to submit an arrangement—don't write a standard (or well-known song). Find a current pop tune that the band doesn't have in its library. If your arrangement is any good at all, they'll be happy to have the tune for free. Then you're in their books and on your way.

So I checked things out, picked out a very forgettable tune called "Pop Goes Your Heart," went back up to Columbia, threw my school books on the floor and wrote the arrangement.

By now the Haymes band was playing at the McAlpin Hotel, and as I approached the dining room where the band played I was confronted by two swinging doors. Not having the money to go in and order dinner, I waited for the pianist—Paul Mitchell—to come out, and pressed my arrangement into his hands. He said, "We'll play it in the next set." I guess that's as excited as I've ever been. There was one problem—I could only hear the band when the swinging doors were open. So I sat there in the lobby—nervous as hell—and waited. From time to time people would enter the dining room. But so far I heard not one note of mine. Then a party of eight entered and I was able to hear my entire introduction to "Pop Goes Your Heart."

A minute passed—the doors swung open again—and they were still playing my song. The doors closed—two minutes went by—they must have finished it by now. The doors opened—they were playing it again. The encouragement this provided sustained me for the next five or six minutes until the band's set was over and Paul Mitchell appeared through the swinging doors. He flashed me the okay sign and said, "You're in!"

It was one of those wonderful moments when you could tell something extraordinary was happening to you even if you weren't quite sure what it was. I was just twenty-two and my life would never be quite the same again.

The Joe Haymes band took the arrangement, "Pop Goes Your Heart," which they didn't pay me for, and asked for an arrangement of "Basin Street Blues," which earned me ten dollars. My third assignment netted me fifteen dollars, but in addition it set in motion a whole new set of circumstances. Lady Luck or Charlie Chance or whatever was at work again.

A third arrangement was a medley of three songs from a then current Broadway show, *Anything Goes*, which included the title song, "I Get a Kick Out of You" and "You're the Top." As the band had a nightly broadcast from the McAlpin I now had a little status with my peers at Columbia. After all, I was "on the radio!" Little did I know that someone far more important than my peers was listening.

In 1934 Rudy Vallée's *Fleischman Hour* was the most prestigious program on the air. It helped to launch the careers of Alice Faye, Edgar Bergen, and Joan Davis among many others. Rudy Vallée heard the Haymes band play the *Anything Goes* medley, and called to ask the name of the arranger. Unfortunately, my name was not mentioned—credit went to someone else. Surprisingly, Lady Luck prompted a trombone player to call me and say, "Hey! Somebody's trying to take credit for your work. Rudy Vallée just called up and asked for the name of the guy who arranged the *Anything Goes* medley." I was pretty naïve then, but at least I was bright enough to write a note to Vallée at Steinway Hall. I mentioned that I had heard he was interested in the medley, that I was the arranger, and that I had the original score if he cared to see it.

The return mail brought a note on elegant stationary, with the name Rudy Vallée rather conspicuous at the top, summoning me with a terse "Be at Steinway Hall at six o'clock on Friday evening." It looked a lot more like a summons than a request, but it looked pretty exciting to me.

At the appointed hour I arrived in the reception room of the Vallée office, not knowing quite what to expect. The outer door opened and a man entered who was wearing dark glasses and was attached to a Doberman Pinscher. Obviously this was a blind man making the rounds of waiting rooms waiting for a handout. I had heard of this practice, but was unaware that a Doberman might be one's choice as an all-purpose seeing-eye dog. At this point in my life I had also never seen anyone other than a blind man wearing dark glasses. So I reached into my pocket, found a quarter, and was about to hand it to this poor unfortunate man when I heard the receptionist say, "Good evening, Mr. Vallée." Needless to say I quickly collapsed into my chair and awaited my summons into the inner sanctum. There sat Rudy Vallée, still in dark glasses, with the Doberman at his side. He said, "I've got a bunch of guys writing arrangements for my orchestra who don't know their ass from their elbow. Would you be interested in working for me on the *Fleischman Hour*?"

Now the Joe Haymes band wasn't exactly chopped chicken, but this was as if someone had said to me "How would you like to play shortstop for the New York Yankees?" I accepted gratefully, got my assignment a day later, and went back up to Columbia and wrote my little heart out. There was a problem. The Haymes band was filled with some of the all-time all-stars as far as musicians were concerned (Bud Freeman on tenor sax, Toots Mondello on alto, Andy Ferretti on trumpet, Ward Sillaway on trombone). I wrote my *Fleischman Show* arrangement as if these men were to play it. The first rehearsal was a disaster. Unbeknownst to me, Vallée's band had a generous percentage of rather pedestrian NBC staff musicians. Halfway through the rehearsal of my first arrangement Rudy fired the whole band. After a hurried conference, cooler heads prevailed and the band was given a reprieve. But a more embarrassing penalty ensued. Vallée sent the whole complement of thirty-five men up to Roseland Ballroom to stand there and listen to the Joe Haymes band play "our" style for an entire evening. My popularity with these musicians couldn't really be measured on a scale of one to ten. After four or five arrangements for Vallée I was only too happy to be asked by Tommy Dorsey to join his arranging staff when he took over the Joe Haymes Orchestra.

The Vallée experience did provide one extremely helpful by-product. All the time I was in New York, drifting ever more helplessly from the academic world into the tainted field of show business, I kept getting reminders from my father in Pittsfield that a Dartmouth economics major should certainly be able to do something more constructive than write music. I was firmly led to believe that I was on the wrong track and had better pull myself together. People would stop him on the street up in Pittsfield and ask just what it was that Paul was doing in New York. When he replied that I was an "arranger" they averted their eyes and shuffled off, certain that the connotation of arranger was a pimp, and that I was busily arranging young girls for elderly men. Quite simply, my father was getting fed up with being felled by Puritanical darts. But the *Fleischman Hour* came to the rescue.

Despite my Ivy League book learning in economics I had not yet dared to attempt the intricacies of a checking account, so the first arranging check with Rudy Vallée's signature was sent back to Pittsfield for safekeeping. It was quite a large check for those days—seventy-five dollars.

My father innocently took it into the Berkshire County Savings Bank, and the sight of Rudy Vallée's autograph suddenly turned the rather dull institution into a madhouse. Lady tellers rushed back and forth, squealing with delight over the Vallée signature. My father became an instant celebrity and I never again heard a discouraging word about show business.

Now let's look back a minute at the consistency of the cliché about being in the right place at the right time. I met Paul Mitchell's mother in Missouri, he advised me to write a standard, Rudy Vallée happened to hear it, the trombone player alerted me, and I showed up at Steinway Hall. And finally Tommy Dorsey decided to take over the Joe Haymes band and me with it!

Six years passed that moment and I'm in Hollywood as an arranger for the Bob Crosby Orchestra. Bing Crosby decided that he'd like to have Bob's band do the musical accompaniment for the motion picture *Holiday Inn*, which he was doing with Fred Astaire. Here I was, on the first job I ever had in Hollywood, arranging all of Fred Astaire's dance numbers and quite a few of the vocals for a picture that is now considered a classic. We had finished the picture and were making the cast record album for Decca, with Victor Young as the musical director. As the arranger I had the opportunity to conduct the rehearsal with the band, while Fred Astaire danced on a four-by-four piece of plywood. When I felt we were ready for a take I signaled for Victor to come into the studio and take over. Instead, he hit the button and said, "No, you've rehearsed it—go ahead and conduct it!"

It was the right time and the right place. I had no track record as a conductor and here I was making a record with Bing Crosby and Fred Astaire. We made the record—it turned out fine—but through the years it wasn't too easy to get nervous over conducting when you'd started out with two real superstars.

Jo Stafford

Like Paul's, my beginning in show business was also rather charmed. My path was never pebbled or prickly but carefully smoothed by my sisters, Christine and Pauline, who were an established duo in radio when I was still in school. I worked with them on occasion but Mama laid down the "rules of the house" for us, and rule number one was that I finish high school and there's no two ways about it.

So I finished my schooling on a Friday, and started work the following Monday morning. My sisters had already hurdled the obstacles and burst the barriers, something I don't think I would have been capable of doing. My inherent shyness probably would have led me to apply for a nice safe job with Mrs. See, selling her chocolate creams.

But fortunately for me, Chris and Pauline were willing to add the high school graduate to their duo, and now there were three—imaginatively called The Stafford Sisters. We were, if I do say so myself, pretty good.

While I certainly couldn't be called a pianist, I could play well enough to help us learn a new song. However, my keyboard insecurity led to some hazardous situations. One I remember—and it still gives me the shakes to think about it—was an audition we went to at radio station KHJ in Los Angeles. The auditions were held in halls big as barns, and appropriately called "cattle calls." There must have been hundreds of people in this huge hall waiting to be auditioned and I felt we'd be lucky if we got to sing the next day, or even the next month.

After several hours of hopefuls trooping in and out of the audition room a rather desperate looking man addressed the group in the waiting room. "Is there anybody here—any act at all—that has their own accompaniment?" I thought to myself, "That leaves us out." But my sister Chris evidently thought otherwise. She stood up and announced, "Oh yes! We have!" My heart sank—she couldn't possibly mean me —but she did.

In we went and auditioned for a small but formidable looking man named J.C. Lewis, Jr. I played the piano nervously, but we sang well. It must have sounded okay because they gave us three fifteen minute shows a week of our own and all because we had our own accompaniment—me. That meant—let's see—four songs a show, three times a week, for a total of twelve arrangements with me thumping out the accompaniments. Not content with our afternoon programs we then got involved with a country music show that went on nightly. That show aired five times a week, plus we tried to fit in a few guest spots and motion picture studio calls singing backgrounds. Sometimes there were too many songs to learn and remember so we'd call in and say Christine had the flu, Pauline had a headache, or I had diphtheria. There was a great casualness about radio then. If we didn't appear there was no panic or hysteria. Someone giving gardening hints or reading highlights of the works of Edgar A. Guest would simply replace us.

It was a good thing we did as many shows as we could because those were the days before any union had established or even suggested a minimum scale. Our salary at first was five dollars per show apiece, but as demand increased, Christine, as our best negotiator, worked our price up to fifteen apiece per show. We made a lively living with mass production.

By now we had a pretty frantic schedule, which involved doing shows very close together time wise, but rather far apart when one considered the location of the studios. Everything was done live, and "you just better be there!" One of our programs, *California Melodies* was done at KHJ, which was located in downtown Los Angeles. *The Chesterfield Supper Club,* broadcast from the Wilshire Ebell Theatre, followed it almost immediately with the star Alice Faye and the Hal Kemp Orchestra. This involved a speedy journey of five miles, accomplished with the help of a motorcycle escort, siren screaming and red light flashing. It was all pretty thrilling for a girl just out of high school. There were ten, eleven radio shows a week, and then came *Alexander's Ragtime Band.*

Just about every group singer and most other professional studio singers as well, worked on the spectacular Twentieth Century-Fox film *Alexander's Ragtime Band.* It wasn't a job; it was more like a career it took so long. The movie starred Tyrone Power, Ethel Merman, Don Ameche, and Alice Faye, who became known as the "Saint of the Singers." If we worked at night and went beyond midnight it became golden time and we were all paid double scale. There were many nights when we were nearing the witching hour and all the cost-concerned minions were rushing us in order to finish up, when Alice Faye would deliberately louse up a take, look over at us with a wink and a grin, and send us into a past-midnight bonanza. Rents were paid in time all over town!

Alexander's Ragtime Band paid off in other dividends as well for me. It was on the set at the studio—sitting around between takes—that I became musically acquainted with The Three Rhythm Kings and The Four Esquires. We started singing together just for fun, and these sessions led to the formation of an eight-voice singing group that we christened The Pied Pipers.

Now another singer working on *Alexander's* was Alyce King of the King family, and it was through Alyce that I was first to meet Paul Weston. Between shooting and recording, The Pied Pipers would invariably find a cozy corner on the lot to work out our vocal arrangements, and one day Alyce happened by and heard what we were up to. Alyce and her sister Vonnie were then dating Paul Weston and Axel Stordahl, two Tommy Dorsey arrangers who were in town while Tommy played at the old Palomar Ballroom. Alyce told them, "You've got to hear this group! They're doing something completely new and they'll knock you out!" Shortly after, Paul and Axel invited the Pipers over for a vocal jam session to hear what all the excitement was about.

Paul

That day when I first heard the Pipers was unlike any other I've ever known. Jack Leonard (Dorsey's vocalist), Herb Sanford (then producing the Raleigh-Kool cigarette program for Tommy), and Axel and I were sharing a small rented house on Colgate Avenue in Beverly Hills. We had set a date to hear these Pied Pipers, whoever they were, and suddenly found our house filled with a large and eager audience of their loyal rooters. Ginny Irwin brought her Music Maids from *The Bing Crosby Kraft Show*, there were also the King Sisters and assorted other singers and friends—all Piper fans. We sat around the house in pleasant anticipation when all of a sudden the Pipers pushed their way through the front door, eight strong, and made a beeline for the kitchen before the introductions were even completed. They hit the refrigerator and ate everything in sight. I remember that they cleaned out our meager supply of catsup and quickly drank all the cooking wine.

When the cupboards were bare they emerged from the kitchen and went into song. Song? There has to be a better word because theirs was a concept of singing we had never heard up until that time. Instead of eight people singing all at once, they worked like a brass section and saxophone section with four voices against four in some really outstanding arrangements. Herb Sanford arrived in the middle of the afternoon and he was impressed as Axel and I were. The Pied Pipers were hired. Although it was not clear then and it's not clear even now whether they were hired by Tommy Dorsey, who had never heard them but took Axel's and my recommendation, or if it was Herb Sanford on behalf of the Raleigh-Kool program. At any rate, because of the afternoon's performance, they were promised *one* radio show in New York.

Jo

Can you imagine eight people piling into a couple of cars and driving three thousand miles from Los Angeles to New York with the premise of doing only one radio show? That's just what we did and you've got to be young to do that—there's no other excuse.

We got there, did our first show and ended up doing seven. Youth was rewarded. Now the head offices of Raleigh-Kool cigarettes, sponsors of Tommy's radio program, were in England, as was the head officer himself, who we'll call Sir Hubert. We never did know his name but he was Sir Something. The American advertising company would record the program each week on a 16-inch transcription disc and send it over to Sir Hubert so he could keep an authoritative ear on the show he was sponsoring in the colonies. But each week, just before mailing the recording, the agency would carefully whack it a few times on the corner of a desk, thereby smashing it into smithereens. The broken record was of course plausible because of the delicate nature of the material and the roughness of the mail handlers. Meanwhile Sir Hubert could be kept from causing any unnecessary interference. The agency was apprehensive that the Tommy Dorsey musical style might be a bit much for Sir Hubert and he might create havoc with demands for Edward Elgar, Gilbert and Sullivan or an occasional love ballad by Ivor Novello. What he didn't know couldn't hurt him and could only help the program.

The tragic undoing of The Pied Pipers as a group of eight took place on the day that Sir Hubert arrived on these shores, unannounced, and made his way directly from ship to studio. Ensconced in the sponsor's booth, separated from us by a thick glass wall, he watched and listened as we were on the air singing with great good cheer, "Hold tight, a-hold tight, hold tight, fododo-de-yacka saki, want some seafood, Mama!" Admittedly the lyrics are unusual, and the Piper arrangement was a little crazier than the lyrics, but we felt that his reaction was uncalled for. About thirty bars into the song he leapt to his feet and started to claw wildly at the glass in the sponsor's booth shouting, "They're mad! Stop them—they're insane! Demented! Get them off my show!!" The thick glass wall prevented his unearthly screams from getting on his program, and sturdy agency personnel held him down until the half-hour was over. The next morning The Pied Pipers were very, very fired.

The abrupt dismissal came at an unfortunate time. It was our first exposure to New York and we were really living it up and loving it. But suddenly here we were in the big cold city without a job. Daily we traveled up and down Broadway, looking woebegone, humble and hungry, hoping someone would hire a group of eight singers to do something or other. Our forays were for naught. We stayed until all we had left was our train fare home, and then we came back to Los Angeles and went on unemployment insurance.

Four of the group had families and decided to seek employment in a less unsteady environment. And with that The Pied Pipers became an unemployed quartette. I received my last check from the government on a Friday from a very formidable bureaucrat who resented giving me the money. I got home somewhat depressed and apprehensive about my future and there was a message for me to call an Operator 82 in Chicago. This mystified me, as I didn't know a living soul in Chicago. But, since the charges were being picked up at the other end, I blithely made the call. The caller was Tommy Dorsey who came right to the point, wasting no time or money and said, "I can't use eight voices, but I would like a quartette with you in it to join the band and be a regular part of the Dorsey organization. What do you say?" I told Tommy that, strangely enough, we were now a quartette and that we'd love to join the band. We'd have joined anything at this point. I made the oral agreement for all of us with no thought to salary, to working hours, transportation or anything else in large or small print.

The early Pied Pipers experiences are another illustration of Paul's and my point that in show business chance is often a significant part of success. It's a wonderful business, but it holds no prophecy, no guarantee, and certainly no opportunity for the careful planning that can promote a business career. Come to think of it, the best thing is to be in the right place at the right time.

Showcasing the stages of shellac record production at a Capitol Records manufacturing plant (ca. March 1946).

Signing autographs at a Capitol Records manufacturing plant (ca. March 1946).

J.S. inspects and autographs her first album release at a Capitol Records manufacturing plant (ca. March 1946).

Left-right. Pauline Stafford, Foster "Ruck" Rucker (a.k.a. Galen Drake), J.S., unknown (ca. 1950). Photograph by Robert Perkins.

The Days of
the Big Bands

Introduction

PAUL

One of the things that has amused Jo and me through the years is the fact that all the books, and the movies and stories about big bands have missed a lot of what really happened during those days. The films about bands were to some extent sugar-coated because a lot of what really took place couldn't be put into a movie. But there were other problems. George Simon, in his excellent book, *The Big Bands*, clearly portrays the ridiculous results of Hollywood directors and writers trying to put on the screen their idea of what went on with the big bands. He tells how, with varying degrees of success, they tried to force band leaders into portraying things they would never have thought of doing on their own.

George was probably the only writer to come close to giving a picture of what life was really like. His is a monumental work of documentation, but his research tended to direct him to recording who played with whom and whose band was the "sweetest" and the "swingingest." He correctly maintains that Tommy Dorsey's band was the greatest combination of both styles ever assembled. But the big band days come forth as being dreadfully serious, and for most of the players and singers those days were anything but that.

Anyone who has been exposed to Billy May's sense of humor, not to mention his great talent, has to wonder what the hell he thought about when he was playing with Glenn Miller. The Glenn Miller story will be gone into later on, but suffice it to say that the Tommy Dorsey gang considered the Miller band to be a really "square" operation. They were commercially a smash, but we always felt that they never swung for more than eight bars at a time. We called them the "boy scouts" and of course at the time we didn't accept the fact that Glenn's insistence on this posture was greatly responsible for their success.

George Simon has told the story of the leaders. But the story of the sideman tells even more about the day-to-day happenings in the times of the big bands. Tommy Dorsey's saga was interesting, but the exploits of his sidemen and singers have to be part of the big band story. Benny Goodman was the subject of many fascinating tales (some of which will not be told here), but his sidemen were characters whose adventures were memorable.

The movies and books have never been able to present an accurate picture of a group of young people working and playing together—on the road most of the time—busily putting down the leader, playing practical jokes on each other night and day, living experiences which seemed a terrible drag at the time, but when looked back on later in life would be judged about as much fun—and sometimes more—than the law allowed.

Big bands were groups of people, and for the most part these people were talented, gentle, endowed with a unique sense of humor, and dedicated to having fun. Being on the road was tough, but every night the band played, the people danced and applauded, and for three or four hours life was about as good as it could ever be. It was a time, like the time of *live* television, that will never happen again, and those who lived it were very fortunate indeed.

Road Managers

PAUL

Many aspects of big band life have never been looked into—for example, the strange adventures of the more colorful road managers. One who comes to mind immediately is Carlos Gastel, Stan Kenton's road manager. Carlos later very effectively managed Nat Cole, Peggy Lee and June Christy, and by rights is worthy of an entire book of his own. He once left for a Peggy Lee opening in Las Vegas via New Orleans, and arrived two weeks later in time for her closing night!

Some managers spent their time searching for gold, some for prestige, but Carlos was bent on searching for recreation. It was an improbable search, and always seemed to lead in the wrong direction. Of all the people you would least imagine putting to sea, Carlos had to head the list. One of his first investments after he touched financial security was a powerboat. Carlos couldn't be bothered with the tiresome details of navigation. He had been told that people with boats went to Catalina Island. One bright, sunny day Carlos very simply took off for Catalina.

I heard the story of his arrival from a seasoned skipper, my good friend Axel Stordahl. I think Ax had been sailing since he was five. He was moored at the isthmus, among a beautiful array of sailing vessels.

You can imagine Axel's dismay one afternoon, near sundown, when over the horizon came this new boat with the robust Carlos Gastel at the helm weaving a rather erratic course towards the isthmus. The bulky body of the skipper, plus the sort of zigzag style of his helmsmanship, would have been enough to call attention to the craft, but in addition Carlos held in his hand a much frowned on, if not forbidden bullhorn.

Carlos at times had a sort of croaking sound to his voice, and the volume he was using really made the bullhorn unnecessary, so the effect was startling, and a definite first for the isthmus. The bullhorn thundered,

"Axel! Axel! Cocktail time. It's cocktail time!"

Axel immediately disappeared below the decks in an attempt to disassociate himself from the oncoming blasts. Cocktail time at the isthmus was always a delightful interlude, but it had never before been announced in such an unrefined fashion. There was further embarrassment in that Carlos was at the helm of a powerboat, and a powerboat at the isthmus was just not yare in those days. The unwritten law demanded that powerboats, with their frivolous, merrymaking crews, go to Avalon. The isthmus was reserved for serious sailors.

As Carlos approached, issuing rather vague instructions to his assistants in a manner that would have revolted the Captain of the Bounty, he gave orders to his first mate to "pick up the mooring." His first mate was called "Big John" and he was a giant of a man who served as both road manager and bodyguard for Nat Cole. Carlos sent him up to "the pointy end" of the boat with a boat hook, told him to watch for the mooring, catch it with the boat hook and thus secure the boat for the festive weekend. Unfortunately, no one had bothered to inform Carlos that slowing the boat down was essential to grappling the mooring. By now he was in among the sloops, yawls, and ketches, his powerboat a lethal weapon, in his own mind certain that something magical would happen when he reached the mooring. With "Big John" alert and poised they approached the mooring at a disastrous rate of speed. "Big John" expertly caught the hook in the anchored mooring and was instantly catapulted into the ocean. That was the end of "Big John's" performance, but Carlos was the closing act. As captain he stayed with his ship, successfully avoided the remaining sailboats, and at a merry pace ran his boat right up on to the beach. His nautical debut was long remembered at the isthmus.

Jo

The adventures of Carlos Gastel on the high seas had a common denominator in that they all flirted with disaster. He had the very bad habit of rounding up his colleagues and starting out for Catalina in the dark of night. This group could hardly be called a crew since there wasn't a trained sailor among them and the mention of a charted course produced furrows and frowns. Invariably Carlos would ask some stranger on the dock, "Which way is Catalina?" and whichever direction a finger pointed became more or less the direct route.

One star-filled night Carlos and his cronies started out and became involved in a hot and heavy poker game. There were five men making the trip and suddenly it was noticed that five men were playing poker, which makes for a good game, but made the journey on the Pacific Ocean a questionable one since no one was at the helm. Someone shouted, "Hey! Who's driving this boat?" and this was followed by a mad rush on deck to assess the situation. Far, far behind them they saw a series of small flickering lights. Someone asked naïvely, "What are those little lights?" All five of them stared at the lights as the boat headed into the unknown. It finally dawned on them that the lights had to be Catalina, and that they were blindly on their way to Japan. A sudden and sober face was made and the Coast Guard was saved a long and tiresome search.

Paul

Another road manager, more staid and conservative than Carlos, but colorful in his own way, was Joe Kearney. Joe had grown up with Bing and Bob Crosby in Spokane, and became road manager for the Bob Crosby Orchestra. This fun-loving group played the best Dixieland music ever turned out by an organized band, and they had a ball on and off the stand. Rounding them up after a night's work and the post-work recreation was Joe's job, and he became acquainted with law enforcement authorities in quite a few cities throughout the country. It was a band that enjoyed elaborate practical jokes played on each other, and it must be acknowledged that despite his responsibility for maintaining decorum and sanity in the organization, Joe Kearney was very much a part of some of these rather childish pranks. On second thought the word childish is ill used, because one episode involved setting up a band member for a false arrest and then going to the jail with instruments and serenading him with "The Prisoner's Song."

I was invited to join the band at Catalina Island in the summer of 1940, and at the end of that summer Joe Kearney announced that he was going to leave the band, go into the seminary, and become a Catholic priest. A development like this in the Tommy Dorsey or Benny Goodman bands would have caused somewhat of a sensation. In the Bob Crosby band it caused scarcely a ripple. As a Catholic from New England I knew one thing—Joe Kearney in his priesthood wasn't going to come up against anything much he hadn't already seen as a road manager in the big band era.

Joe went through his training, was ordained, and became the head of the Catholic Labor Institute during a difficult time in the Archdiocese of Los Angeles. After spending quite a few years doing missionary work in Peru, he found time to officiate at Jo's and my wedding and perform the baptismal for both of our children.

When he first came out of the seminary he was asked about his plans. His brother had been quite a famous missionary in China, and people wondered if he was going to follow in his brother's footsteps. At the time Joe replied that instead he thought he'd get a trailer and follow the Bob Crosby band around. He allowed as to how "there was much more work to be done there than there was in China."

The High and Low Roads of Bobby Burns

PAUL

Bobby Burns and I were classmates at Dartmouth College. We graduated in 1933, but Burns exhibited his show business acumen very early in his collegiate life. At the time I had a band called The Green Serenaders. We were a pretty solid outfit, but existed in the shadow of the Barbary Coast Orchestra—Dartmouth's famous dance band. I wasn't a good enough piano player to make the Barbary Coast, which was a great disappointment at the time, but turned out to be fortunate in light of later developments. Burns used our band as the base for one of his ideas, a really crafty scheme.

Hanover, New Hampshire, was not a town known for its many female occupants. There were just the daughters of the townspeople and the daughters of the faculty who were usually let out only in the daytime with chastity belts firmly attached. The town had this little hall over on the south side and Burns made arrangements to rent it on Saturday nights. He would spend the day going round town, inviting every available girl to come to the hall on Saturday night as his guest. He got some lovely ones; some semi-hookers, some turkeys, but he did get the entire female population of Hanover inside the hall.

In order to get a date on Saturday night the students of Dartmouth College had to stand clamoring at the door of the hall. It was the only way they were going to let off steam, sew a few wild oats or even get near a woman on the particular evening. The charge for each student to release his pent up energy was one dollar. Burns stood at the front of the hall collecting the cash. He took in over two hundred dollars out of which he paid fifteen for rent. Meanwhile the band, which included the leader, got three dollars each. The rest went into Bobby Burns' pocket, which wasn't a bad haul at all. We were too dumb to add up the figures and ask for a bigger share.

Another classic story of the enterprising Burns concerns an old, very old building in Hanover that was called, not too surprisingly, the Old White Church. It was built sometime during the 19th century. One night the dry, crisp wood of the church caught on fire. The flames started shooting up, coloring the campus with a tomato red glow. The students, as a body, came surging out of the dorms to watch the holy conflagration. Everybody ran towards the church, Burns ran in the opposite direction. With the speed of a pursued jackrabbit, Burns ran downtown and bought up all the ice cream, popsicles and cold soda he could carry. The fire was hotter than hell, everyone was sweating and close to melting and here comes Burns milling through the crowd yelling, "Get your ice cream here…ice cold sodas…popsicles…ice cream…" And on the night of the big fire Burns made another modest fortune. He was sharp then.

Burns was really something else with Tommy Dorsey. He'd been with the band, as road manager, for about a year and a half and at the time he was back to struggling—he had little or no money. We were playing at the Pennsylvania Hotel in New York and, after the session, everyone was down at Kelly's bar. That is everyone except Tommy who was in his hotel room fast asleep. No pain was felt at Kelly's bar. Between drinks someone asked Burns if he had any money in the bank. As a gag he showed them his bankbook number that was 39342. Of course it had nothing to do with what he had in his account. One of the fellows in the band, with bleary eyes, saw the figure and blurted, "Hey, Burns has over thirty-nine thousand dollars in the bank." Compared to today that was like having three hundred and ninety thousand dollars. Edythe Wright, the girl singer, a self-appointed Mata Hari, scurried to a phone, woke Tommy Dorsey out of a sound sleep and screamed, "Bobby Burns has thirty-nine thousand dollars in the bank!" Without a pause, as sturdy as if he had already had eight hours sleep, Tommy screamed back, "The son of a bitch stole it from me!"

To Tommy there was just no other way Burns could have that much money. The situation became, within seconds, a hornet's nest. The next day there was a kangaroo court and Burns was summoned to appear before Tommy. Burns kept muttering that he didn't have any money in the bank but Tommy was adamant. He glared at Burns and made this thunderous pronouncement, "I know for a fact—for a fact, that you have over thirty-nine thousand dollars in the bank and you—you're not only fired, but you are banished from New York City."

Think about that for a moment. How can a bandleader tell someone they are banished from New York City? Burns took it to heart, packed up and went back home to Syracuse. Later, when a little cool set in, Axel Stordahl and I went to Tommy and told him the true story. Tommy listened, paced the floor, thought silently, turned and with furrowed brows said, "I am not going to rehire him. No, I'm not." There was a dramatic pause, "but he can come back to New York!"

Burns was notified that he would not be rehired, but that Tommy granted him permission to return to New York. We were playing the Paramount Theatre when he came back. He'd stand sheepishly in the dark doorway across the street from the stage door and as we came out, after a performance, we'd spy him and go over and talk with him so he wouldn't feel too cracked up about not being with the band. Eventually Tommy saw the full error of his way and Bobby Burns was rehired. The incident is, perhaps, the first and only time in history that a bandleader banished a man from a whole city.

P.W. and Nat "King" Cole (mid-1940s).

Peggy Lee makes a guest appearance on Paul's CBS radio show (October 26, 1951).

Capitol Records publicity photo (late-1940s).

First glamour portrait (ca. 1944). Photograph by Ted Allan.

The Dorsey Years

The Battle of the Dorseys

PAUL

One thing I'm very grateful for is the opportunity I had to work and live through the era of the big bands. At times I feel very sorry for youngsters coming up in the entertainment industry who can't have the chance to enjoy the training that these bands afforded. The celebrated "battle of the Dorseys" was a great break for me. The Dorsey Brothers Orchestra had been playing at Glen Island Casino and a long smoldering dispute between Tommy and Jimmy was fanned into a rather exciting blow-up one night over something as simple as the proper tempo for a dance number. Jimmy had been fronting the band—standing up while Tommy sat down in the trombone section. Tommy was too much of the leader type for this arrangement to work for very long anyway. When the final blowup came Tommy decided to organize his own band and Jimmy took the nucleus of the Dorsey Brothers group to California to work with Bing Crosby on his radio show.

Tommy looked around for an organized group to front, and his unerring eye for talent fell on Joe Haymes and His Orchestra. Joe Haymes was probably one of the most underappreciated bandleaders of the big band era. He always had a band with a fine sound, great soloists and fine arrangements, but the band never made it with the public. Joe himself was a fine arranger and wrote for saxophones as well as anyone I ever met, but he wasn't a forceful personality, and the takeover of his band by Tommy, while it started with much promise of mutual benefits, wound up in pretty much of a hassle with everyone mad at everyone else.

The Song of the Open Road

Paul

I was with the Dorsey band before Jo, at a time when the band was impoverished. There wasn't enough money in the till to hire a Greyhound bus, so Tommy took the meager resources and bought a second hand, maybe third hand bus from Father Divine who was then the world's leading preacher man. We didn't have a driver, but we did have Joe Bauer, the third trumpet player, who voted himself, unanimously, as the driver. The guys in the band were as scared as kids getting vaccinated for the first time. Joe had a reputation for being unstable on the ground, let alone on something moving. Every time he got behind the wheel he would yell, "Here we go!" and charge forward up the highway at eighty miles an hour in this shaky, decrepit bus that the band soon named the Silver Bullet. We were lucky to get from one place to another without loss of life or limb or both.

Tommy was completely unworried by the numerous breakdowns and the reckless speed at which his bus was driven, since he usually traveled by car and was normally sound asleep at the hotel by the time the Silver Bullet completed the night's journey. The band would finish playing around midnight, pack up and board the Silver Bullet, and drive perhaps three hundred miles to the next job. Those lucky enough to be able to sleep on the bus would not be too badly off, but any sensible soul, aware of the dangerous conditions under which he was being propelled across the country, would be unable to close an eye until he reached the next stop, where there might be time for a nap before getting ready for the nightly job.

As the band gained fame and economic security, it graduated to Greyhound buses and uniformed drivers and at times Tommy took to riding the bus, with rather interesting results. With Tommy on the bus, the rebels sought sanctuary at the extreme rear, where they could plot against the leader and consume whatever they felt they needed to fortify them against the long ride and Tommy.

One of the favorite ploys was "putting Tommy on"—this took several interesting forms. Tommy, with the help of five arrangers, had conceived and developed the arrangement of "Song of India," which of course was a big hit and was Tommy's pride and joy. The renegades would wait until things were relatively quiet in the bus and then sing a dreadful parody of the "Song of India" arrangement, while Tommy would sit up front and really steam.

Another ploy was "looking for the Hindenburg." Tommy might be in an expansive and friendly mood on certain nights, particularly after the band had drawn a big crowd and played well, and when this mood was upon him he would stand at the front of the bus, facing the rear, and tell numerous stories concerning his early days when he played with Bix Beiderbecke and the famous Jean Goldkette band. These stories were reasonably amusing, but the band had heard them quite a few times and the humor of them diminished accordingly. Therefore the stories came to be looked on as being about as funny as the Hindenburg disaster. So as soon as Tommy would start the stories, the renegades would start looking skyward as if they were "looking for the Hindenburg." Tommy never really knew what was going on, and might not have even cared, but the renegades drew great solace from their little joke and it was the cause of much snickering after the story period was over.

Jo

Bus drivers were sitting ducks and unsung heroes. We'd go out on the road for three and four weeks at a time, always using the same bus and bus driver. The driver would arrive at the beginning of the tour, immaculately uniformed hat perked at the correct angle, sporting a "take charge" attitude not unlike that of the Captain of a German U-boat. Invariably these drivers were choked up with the excitement at the prospect of driving a big band around the country. We put those poor men through sheer hell. They would have been safer in a German U-boat in either Work War I or II. Touring on a bus with a big band was purely and simply, the pits. Whoever said, "War is hell," never toured with a band.

Like Count Dracula we all had a strange urge to be abed before dawn—an urge rarely satisfied. The length of the bus trip determined when we would arrive at our destination and most of the time we'd get to our hotel rooms at ten or eleven in the morning—and so to bed. We didn't spend a lot of money on sun tan lotion. The times when we went to sleep by the "light of the silvery moon" were few and consequently a much looked forward to happening.

With this in mind we determined that the first responsibility of the bus driver was to navigate the trips keeping in mind that the shortest distance between two points is a straight line. There were times when this simple logic did not prevail.

This one night we were scheduled to wind up in Altoona, Pennsylvania. The hop was a mere two hundred and fifty miles, a really short hop. The heaven of a haven was in sight. We were going to get there in time to find a hotel room and lie down in an honest-to-goodness bed before dawn. But it wasn't in the cards. Somehow, somewhere, this poor soul bus driver lost Altoona. He lost it! We just drove in great, narrowing circles, not around Altoona, not even near it.

We should have arrived at, say four-thirty in the morning. Well it became five, six-thirty, seven o'clock and we were still roaming in the gloaming. It was a weird hour for a prank, but that's when weird ideas seem to be born. We decided to punish the lost driver. We made him stop the bus and we all tromped out and, with bold, artistic flourishes, painted a big sign across the side of his bus that read, "Altoona or Bust!" We forced him to drive with that reminder of our lost night for the rest of the trip. He did finally get us into Altoona. How he managed to find it I have no idea and when I saw it I was not too thrilled, but by the time he discovered it we were robbed of that longed for bath and bed.

Another unforgettable chapter in our life with our bus driver happened in Tennessee where, when it rains, it pours. It was during one of these deluges that we were creeping through the night and came face to face with a rickety old bridge. The driver halted the bus with his familiar abruptness and came to a dead, body-jolting stop. The rain was a wall of water. We had all had him up to our necks by this time and when he stood up and announced, "I've got to have some help here, because I don't know if this bridge is safe for us to cross. The river is rising and I have to go out there and test it." Well, we just sat there, unmoving and said, "Testing is the bus driver's job." The defeated, abject look appeared as he said, "I can't drive the bus and test the bridge too." We told him, "You can test and *then* drive the bus." He got no help from us. Knowing he was outnumbered and in a pitiful minority, he went out into the wet world and walked slippingly across the bridge. We sat there and watched him, not caring if he disappeared into the torrent. As far as we were concerned we left the driving and the testing to him.

I'll never forget one of my arrivals at a campus, the campus of the University of Georgia. We had just finished another of those delightful trips they used to dream up for us. It was one of the seven hundred milers. We were booked to do a tea dance at four o'clock in the afternoon and go straight into a dance that night. As the bus pulled up to the campus, with its Tommy Dorsey and his Orchestra sign in front, "Altoona or Bust!" on the side, half the students gathered around to welcome us. I'd been on this damned bus all night long, pulled together like a stale pretzel. I remember when I got off, hair in curlers, no makeup, dress hanging over my arm, a campus "biggie" with terminal acne and a loud voice queried, "My God, is that Jo Stafford?" I was so pooped at the time I didn't even care. I just marched grandly through the crowd.

As the days went by the driver became scragglier looking. He lost his hat, discarded his tie and kept staring into vacant air like a possessed owl. Another night, again a short trip, we were someplace in the wilds of Ohio. Short trips were his nemesis, his downfall. It was in this small Ohio town, smack in the center of a residential street, when the bus broke down. We all sat there in the dark while our not too beloved driver was out trying to fix whatever was wrong with the motor. No luck. Dawn comes up, people are waking in their little square white houses and by now we were so frustrated that the fellows in the back of the bus took out a couple of seats: Buddy Rich got hold of his drums; a few horn players got their instruments; and there, in the middle of this tiny town, on this quiet residential street, they started jamming and serenading the rising sun. The townsfolk popped their heads out of their bedroom windows with expressions of terror and shock. I guess it didn't seem unreasonable to them—what with the dawn and the din that this was the day Gabriel and the Saints were marching into Ohio…and maybe, just maybe, they were in Heaven instead of Ohio.

We were eventually rescued, but not until another bus arrived from Cleveland, several hours later. Our bus driver, his last name was King, took on the bedraggled look of the Count of Monte Cristo just before he dug his way out. He was a disgusted and unhappy man. On our way back to New York, ambling along someplace in New Jersey we decided we were really fed up with him and wanted revenge.

So, Sinatra, Joe Bushkin, and George Arus, always on deck when it came to something evil, went up front while King was driving and totally defenseless. They took the pen he used to make his markings, his maps and whatever else a bus driver carries and threw everything out of the window chanting, "If he can't find Altoona, he'll never find New York. So what does he need this stuff for?" I heard later that when the driver returned to his headquarters he went directly to his boss and begged, literally pleaded, to never, never again be sent out with those crazy people.

Paul

Bus trips were something else. I think one of the craziest stories of a Dorsey bus trip was one where the band was coming back from some place in the South. Tommy had a habit, if the band didn't play well in the last set, or if someone displeased him during the evening, of not allowing the band to eat after the job before they got on the bus. He would also command the driver to drive the bus straight ahead without allowing any pee stops. Tommy apparently had strong kidneys and his anger with the band overcame his desire to go to the bathroom. So it was "straight ahead driver" through the night.

The evil ones would always gather in the back of the bus. The fiddle players, if any, were always up front, then the saxophone players, next came the trombone players and in the back sat the trumpet players. They were the most evil. This one saxophone player had a raccoon coat, full length, not knee length but full to the floor. It was a college fashion back in 1936. He didn't go to college, but he did have the coat.

He was in the back of the bus on this noted night with the evil ones, drinking beer. In those days a beer can didn't have a flip top opening. You had to use a can opener, cutting a triangular hole in the can. They were all merrily cutting triangles and guzzling beer. Cans were rolling up and down the aisle of the bus and as the night wore on, the urge to go to the bathroom began to really assert itself. Finally, the saxophone player couldn't stand it anymore. He went up to the front of the bus, tapped Tommy on the shoulder, and asked if they could please have a pee stop. Tommy, being in his dark mood, said, "No way. Straight ahead driver." And on the bus went.

The sax player stumbled to the back of the bus and resumed cutting triangles and guzzling beer. He was okay for a time, maybe about six minutes. After a couple more beers he began to get desperate. Everyone knew Tommy would not stop so they decided the troubled saxophone player should pee into a beer can. It was a last ditch effort and he carefully inserted his organ into the triangular hole of the beer can and sighed, knowing relief was in sight and the problem was in the can. The bus was jiggling, the sharp edged hole was triangular, but the sax player wasn't. It was a case of a round peg in an angular hole. He managed, what with that jiggling and irritation, to get an erection, which immediately trapped him inside the beer can. Peeing was not the problem, survival was. Everyone began turning cold sober. Here was this poor victim with a beer can stuck on the end of his tallywacker.

Feeling great sympathy, the fellows formed a delegation and stalked up to see Tommy. They told him, "There's a bad thing going on in the rear of the bus. One of the guys has a beer can stuck on the end of his john. We gotta do something." Tommy said, "That's his problem. Straight ahead driver."

By now the sax player was letting out screams of, "It's bleeding! It's bleeding!" The delegation grew in numbers and again went to Tommy with the proclamation, "It's bleeding! It's bleeding! We have got to stop the bus!"

At this point the bus had traveled far enough up North so that the ground was white with snow. The delegation explained that rubbing snow on the player's injured member was the only possible solution to this appalling problem.

Tommy was made clearly aware of the seriousness of the situation and of "the imperiled penis." He agreed to stop the bus. The delegation went to the back of the bus, took the sax player's raccoon coat, wrapped it around him, the beer can and his you-know-what. He trundled up the aisle, eased himself ever so gently down the steps, grabbed snow and rubbed it all over the injured area until he was able to make a safe withdrawal. He climbed back into the bus and this time the order of "straight ahead driver" sounded beautiful.

Another classic of the early days of the Dorsey band was the story of Davie Tough. He was one of the greatest jazz drummers of all time and a small, gentle, talented man who really sparked the band. He was very intelligent and tremendously well read. When the others were buried in comics and racing forms, Davie was buried between the hard covers of the classics. This was a period when the general level of learning could provoke a controversy about billboards passed along the road with the argument being, "Did that tobacco sign say mail pouch or mail pooch?"

We had a trumpet player in the band who got involved in Chicago with a movie star. It's better not to use their names since they're both alive and will readily recognize themselves. They fell madly in love at first sight and it was one of the most romantic affairs of the century. The sad moment came when the band had to leave Chicago and the star said to the trumpet player, "You be sure and let me hear from you because we're in love and will love each other from this time on forever. But I've got to have a constant demonstration of your love from me."

The band headed West with Des Moines as the first stop. The trumpet player started getting a little tense about sending out a "constant demonstration." He went to Davie Tough and said, "Look, I've got this movie star in Chicago and she expects to hear something from me. Would you write out a telegram that I could send her that would show my love for her?" Davie said he would give it some thought. He never believed in starting at the bottom, so he began with Elizabeth Barrett Browning. The first telegram was "How do I love thee? Let me count the ways." A perfect ten-word wire and you can safely bet neither the trumpet player nor the movie star knew where the line came from. This thing hit Chicago and the movie star went right up into the air, this was one of the greatest tributes she's ever read. She thought the guy was great in person and even better in his telegraphed demonstrations. The telegram put her away. She wired back, "I cannot believe the wonderful message. More! More! More! More!" Again, exactly ten words. At the trumpet player's request, Davie furnished more, more, more. He branched out into Edna St. Vincent Millay, Shakespeare, Rosetti, the Bible...and telegrams were arriving at regular intervals. The movie star was fractured. She pleaded for the musician to keep the wires flowing. She could not believe how much she loved him. It was the Cyrano story reenacted in all its glory.

Then a terrible thing happened. Tommy Dorsey and Davie Tough had a big fight and Davie was fired and out of town in twenty-four hours. This was catastrophic. It got worse. Six days passed without the trumpet player wiring a single word. The movie star sent repeated messages, "Where are my telegrams? Do you still love me? What happened to our romance? What happened to your demonstrations?"

The trumpet player was beside himself and in absolute desperation. In his very own words, which I thought very dear and very tender, he explained his final dilemma, "I didn't know what to do. I looked all through the newspapers and couldn't find a single poem." It was funny and sad and a different ending to the Cyrano story. But it sure was an ending to the trumpet player's romance.

As I said before, my trips with the band were somewhat limited. I was able to stay in the sane and safe security of New York and mail my arrangements out. I never graduated from a bus to the luxury of a train like Jo did.

Jo

We began traveling by train after Tommy hired—I forget how many strings—but the organization at this point got up to thirty or more people. Travel by train was utter luxury, but despite the room, we were again divided into our front of the bus, back of the bus formation. There was one car where the fiddle players and the saxophone players hung out and in the other were the brass, The Pied Pipers and other evil people.

There was one calamitous night when I would have been smart if I had joined the violin players. We were on our way to Austin, Texas, and I was elate with the prospect of lying down, even if it was to be in a rocking berth. I got ready for bed very early. My hair, again up in curlers, no makeup, a fresh, clean nightgown and a promise of pleasant sleep there in my lower kingdom. I got in and snapped the curtains shut. I breathed in purring sighs. At that very moment the evil ones, the male Pipers, the brass section, the trombone players, Sinatra and Tommy got into a water fight. They began tossing water at each other out of Dixie cups. They were thundering up and down the aisle, loud laughs and shrill screams crowding the air. I snuggled in my berth, pretending they weren't there. I didn't have a chance. The mad cacophony began to sound like a replay of the Charge of the Light Brigade.

During the melee the train got into San Antonio and we had to layover for three hours. We were to stay in the cars and be switched up to another engine that would take us on to Austin. We were shoved to a siding and there we lay. Instead of carrying on inside the train, the boys could now take up their fight outside and the ammunition changed from water to whiskey. I kept ignoring them and tried to sleep. I was doing fairly well, had fallen into that first, rewarding rest, when I was brought to by a scratching on the curtains of my berth. It turned out to be old Tommy, pretty smashed and in need of conversation. I unbuttoned the snaps; he then sat on the edge of the berth and told me how excited he was that his new girlfriend was showing up tomorrow in Austin—information that just thrilled me to death. He was buried in sloshing sentiment and his romantic revelations left me with an icy indifference. I guess he sensed my lack of sympathy, because he left me suddenly and joined the whiskey throwers. The fight was still raging.

I re-buttoned the snaps on the berth, found a comfortable niche in the pillow and was brought up again by an agonized yell, which I recognized as one of The Pied Pipers. His terrified cry echoed up and down the train. He screamed, "I can't see! I'm going blind! Help me!" Someone—and I think it was Tommy—had thrown a full Dixie cup of whiskey into John Huddleston's eyes. I was married to John at the time and got frantic when I realized what had happened. John came staggering to me, arms outstretched, sobbing, "I am blind. I cannot see. I am blind." I was well aware that he was "blind," but I hadn't yet connected his problem with his eyes.

I jumped up and put on a robe. Unfortunately, I was bewildered as to what to do since it was only four o'clock in the morning. Ziggy Elman, God rest his soul, took us both out and packed us into a taxi. I asked the driver to take us to the nearest emergency hospital. When we walked into the hospital, the nurse looked at us and asked, "Are you by any chance with the Tommy Dorsey Orchestra?" Seems we were the third ones in that night, but ours was the first case of "blinded by bourbon."

The doctor washed John's eyes, bandaged them and I got us a cab to go back to the train station. It's now about five-thirty in the morning. We got out of the cab and as I was leading blind John through the station, I noticed our train car was not there. Here I am staggering around, John, still smashed, is leaning on me. To add to the drama I am not a very poetic picture in my robe and curlers.

After questioning everyone in sight I was told the train had been taken off the siding and was located somewhere in the dark recesses of the railroad yards. It was an impasse of the worst kind. I couldn't very well stumble over tracks and switches with this helpless, drunken, blind man attached to me. I was disgusted, so thoroughly disgusted I just sat down on a bench. I sat there with John at my side feeling like a mangy, untrained Seeing Eye dog. We sat there for about an hour and during those tense sixty minutes John never—not once—did he stop muttering and whining, "I'm blind. I can't see." My sympathy had worn thin by now. At six-thirty people were beginning to come into the station to start their day – the workers and commuters appearing in full force. And this was the very moment John chose to start throwing up. It was done in perfect rhythm, a heavy heave every ten seconds. It was so desperate, so tragic, so humiliating, and so damned dumb. I thought, "I'm not going to be embarrassed." I decided if people came up to me and asked what I was doing, I'd just sit there, stare them down with an attitude reflecting the words of a former Queen of England—"We are not amused!"

Frank Sinatra

Jo

We were playing at the Palmer House in Chicago—the same place where The Pied Pipers joined the band. The male vocalist was in the process of leaving and we were about to pick up a new one in Milwaukee. It was our last night there and we left by train from Chicago and arrived in Milwaukee fairly early in the morning. Tommy was scheduled to rehearse with the new boy singer before the show. The other vocalists didn't have to be at the rehearsal, so we never saw or heard the new boy singer. The Pied Pipers were on stage for the entire show so the first we saw of the new vocalist was when Tommy introduced him.

The first show was always around eleven in the morning, which is not an hour conducive to great enthusiasm in musicians. None of us paid any attention to the introduction. We'd been through it too many times. This kid walked out, a fairly average looking kind of guy, totally unprepossessing. We all felt blasé and sort of "Okay fella, what is it you do?" He walked out and started to sing "Stardust." All I can tell you is that eight bars into the song every head popped up. I don't know how to explain it really, but I was aware that I was hearing something absolutely new—absolutely unique.

No one anywhere, ever sounded like that. He was a pure, unadulterated original. Most male singers, if they had a goal, wanted to sound like Bing Crosby. This young man was not sounding like Crosby. He sounded like no one I had ever heard before. I knew in just those eight bars that here was a memorable voice, but of course at that time I had no idea how famous it was to become.

Paul

I left the band in 1940 at around the same time that Jack Leonard left. After Jack, Tommy went through a long succession of singers. I merely decided after five years with Tommy that I wanted to branch out. So I left to become Dinah Shore's conductor. Tommy, I recall, wished me well and told me about this guy he'd found who was coming in to sing. Tommy said he thought the fellow was pretty good and that his name was Frank Sinatra. I replied, "Sinatra? Frank Sinatra?" I looked at Tommy and with great wisdom said, "Tommy, my advice to you is this. The first thing, the very first thing you have to do is change the name. With a name like that he'll never make it." Tommy listened to me and said, "We'll see." I always thought this was an all-time high for dumb advice, but I did learn thirty years later from George Simon's book that Harry James also wanted to change Frank's name. Frank's talent made the whole matter rather academic.

An Embarrassing Moment

Jo

Whenever a band was out on the road for two or three weeks it would come to New York City to combine record dates with an appearance at the Paramount or Capitol Theatre. Making such an appearance was always a kind of jolt because the one-nighters were late night things and we were all geared to not going to bed before dawn. At the Paramount the first show was always around ten-thirty in the morning. Waking up early and facing the light of day is usually an insurmountable task for a musician. It was a drag.

The opening day show was an exception to the rule. It was always stimulating watching the new dance act or listening to the new comedian. They kept you awake. But after a few days, when the routines became familiar and you knew the dance steps by heart, well, then inertia set in. Knowing what's next takes away any excitement. There was always the chance of maybe being a little hung over. The Pied Pipers, as I mentioned before, stayed on stage during the performance. They sat directly behind the saxophone section.

Freddie Stulce, our first sax player, had marvelous hands. I used to take my shoes off during the acts and when Freddie wasn't playing, he'd massage my feet, something that I dearly loved. This is exactly what happened during one of those early morning shows and it lulled me, lulled me into a deep sleep. There I was, conked out when one of the Nicholas Brothers, Harold, spotted me as he turned around during his routine. He stopped dancing and brought my inert, slumped body to Tommy's attention. Tommy, thank God, had a great sense of humor about my being asleep and he stopped the show and signaled to the man in the booth to throw a glaring spotlight on me. There was a tomblike silence. The stillness woke me. I slowly opened my eyes, bathed in this powerful light, and saw the band, the Pipers, Tommy, the Nicholas Brothers and two thousand five hundred people staring at me. I stared back like a mindless idiot. To my surprise, I got a standing ovation!

The Leader

PAUL

I've always had tremendous admiration for Tommy Dorsey. As a leader he demanded absolute perfection. He was understanding if a man did his best and missed a note or two; but he did not understand if someone was sloppy. Sloppiness was one thing he could not and would not abide. If there was a break in a number, a two bar break, and someone played through it, there was a twenty-five dollar fine. One of the guitar players who'd been with the band for about two weeks left for another job. After he'd gone we looked over his music and he had written on one of the pages, "Watch out! Twenty-five dollars!" Inefficiency and inattention were things Tommy would not tolerate.

JO

Tommy had more than a desire for perfection; he had a need of it. I've talked to a lot of people who read him off, complained about his Irish temper and his tirades, but during the three years I was with the band, I never had any problems with Tom, not one. He was a true artist and a marvelous teacher. He demanded excellence. He gave it and wanted it in return. He would never ride a guy for a reed squeak or an honest mistake. If it was unintentional and funny, he'd laugh as loud and as long as anyone else.

PAUL

There were many leaders in the big band days who were easier to work for than Tommy Dorsey, but none with whom the experience could be more valuable. Watching him take the band through a new arrangement or conduct a radio program rehearsal taught me things I was able to use throughout my professional life. He was a self-taught conductor, but had the ability of making musicians perform at the top of their capabilities.

If Tommy's abilities and creative energies had been directed toward music alone his life would surely have been more tranquil, but his Irish imagination often led him into quixotic adventures. It was as if the "little people" periodically suggested to him bizarre schemes for the band, involving oil wells, a music magazine, communal living, and even a mass enlistment in the U.S. Navy. These episodes, plus some peccadilloes of various sidemen in some of the other big bands will be detailed in later chapters.

P.W. with his close friend and colleague James B. Conkling (mid-1940s).
Photograph by Curtis Studios L.A.

P.W. and Axel Stordahl with an unidentified man (late-1930s).

Photograph by Ray Whitten (ca. 1948).

Publicity photograph for the American Folk Songs album (1948).

In the recording studio with the Pied Pipers (ca. 1943).

The Business of Music

Tin Pan Alley

PAUL

One of the most interesting characters to ever inhabit Tin Pan Alley was Dave Clark. Dave was a songwriter whose lyrics defy description. At first they seem to make very little sense, but repeated listening reveals the ideas behind them. Nevertheless, Dave sang them with all the assurance of a Sammy Cahn. Here's a fine example:

> Way down South in Georgia,
> was the name they knew the place.
> No matter what the colors meant,
> in every Southern race.

In the late thirties Dave must have been around seventy years of age, and he would wander through the Brill building each afternoon, putting a small hit on a few of his many "friends," and perhaps doing a couple of performances in case a group happened to be gathered in one of the publisher's offices. In the evening he sat in his own office, a fire plug against the wall next to Lindy's restaurant, and hailed songwriters and publishers as they emerged, picking up a five here, a ten there, and thus earning his living. Irving Berlin never failed him, and when he was in New York from his songwriting chores in Hollywood, Harry Warren made his contribution and incidentally became the only man I ever met who could play and sing most of Dave's songs.

Dave did have some degree of mental incapacity, perhaps the result of an infectious disease contracted in his younger days, and he presented his songs at the piano with great seriousness, unmindful of smiles and other expressions of delight that might be evident behind his back. Like the rule of Metropolitan Opera buffs at a Florence Foster Jenkins concert that you could never laugh aloud, we were made aware early on that we should never laugh at one of Dave's performances, no matter how provocative the lyrics.

One of his biggest "hits" was a song he wrote after a speaker at an ASCAP dinner gave a talk that was much too long, with too many statistics, and quite a few statements that Dave found difficult to understand. Here is the first verse:

> He's too persistent to me, hah hah
> With numbers as foolish can be, hah hah
> It seems like the numbers were painted on seas,
> And I was impressed to the tops of the trees.
>
> He's too persistent for me, hah hah
> Was never a man like he, hah hah
> Of all the expressions the world seems concessions,
> He's too persistent for me, hah hah.

Dave was a true Tin Pan Alley character and I hope that somewhere someone has all his songs carefully written down. They're certainly unique. Here's "Lindy Lou," another favorite:

> Lindy Lou, Lindy Lou,
> that's all they know his name.
> Lindy Lou, Lindy Lou,
> the new moon like sugar cane.
> The echoes of the valley moon,
> sounds his voice like tender tune
> Ding Dong, Ding Dong, Ding Dong, Ding Dong
> He was known as Lindy Lou.

In the thirties and forties the big bands were given much attention by the music publishers and songwriters since they had radio broadcasts all through the week and thus, even more than through their recordings, brought a new song to the attention of the American public. And as arrangers for the Tommy Dorsey Orchestra, Axel Stordahl and I were probably thought to have more influence than Tommy in picking tunes for the band to play than we really did. In light of later stories about payola I guess we were either naïve or too honest for what was to happen in future years, but aside from gifts of cologne and travel clocks at Christmas we never profited from our position. In addition, Tommy just wouldn't play a song he didn't like and Axel and I knew better than to try to convince him to play a tune that he considered a "dog."

Speaking of "dogs," Tommy was particularly critical of the songs then published by Shapiro-Bernstein. The firm leaned heavily to western material, like "Heading for the Last Roundup," "Take Me Back To My Boots," and "Saddle." And the idea of getting this type of song into Tommy Dorsey's band library was pretty ridiculous. Nevertheless Jonie Taps, the Shapiro-Bernstein number one music man would never miss a night coming into whatever hotel Tommy's band was playing in. This faithfulness was rewarded in a most disgraceful way. As soon as Jonie appeared, as he walked to Tommy on the bandstand, Tommy would interrupt whatever was going on—a vocal or instrumental solo or even a trombone solo by Tommy himself, and actually bark at Jonie until he mercifully reached his table. Of course the band thought it was great fun, but it must have appeared pretty mysterious to the dancers and diners.

Axel and I spent many of our afternoons hanging out at Remick Music, where "The Mouse" Warren was head man, or professional manager as the title went. Jimmy Van Heusen, yet to attain his great fame as a songwriter, was the house piano player, who would rehearse Remick songs with singers who might be liable to perform them on the radio. The Mouse, who was Harry Warren's brother, was small but feisty, and was the only man I've ever known who thought of the best way to keep his head down during a golf swing. He had "head" printed on the toe of his left golf shoe, and "down" printed on the right toe in letters almost an inch high. And he played pretty well!

The Mouse had one trick he loved to pull that now seems a bit on the cruel side, but at the time seemed like great fun. A young singer with one of the lesser bands used to make periodic visits to the Mouse's office, and the Mouse and Jimmy and those of us hanging around there would participate in "recording" sessions where this singer would rehearse him carefully. Then when he was ready to record, the Mouse would buzz his secretary after telling the singer to begin recording when he heard two buzzes. The secretary, in on the gag, would buzz twice, the singer would step up to the wall thermometer, which he thought was a microphone, and sing two choruses with all the emotion he could muster. At a later date when he asked to hear the recording he'd be told it hadn't turned out well, and he'd be ready to go again a month or two later.

Next door to Remick was Whitmark Music, where Ken Lane (later to gain fame on TV as Dean Martin's pianist) had the same job as Van Heusen at Remick. Two singers loved to rehearse with him, but he often kept one of them waiting for hours while he rehearsed with Nan Wynn, who was on the CBS network. The waiting singer finally got tired of waiting and went over to Robbins where she started rehearsing with their pianist, Ticker Freeman. Her name was Dinah Shore, and Ticker was with her for most of her well-documented career.

Ticker was a great practical jokester, and figured in the trials and tribulations of a New Yorker who moved to California and whom I'll call "The Songwriter." The Songwriter had literally never been off cement in his life until he came West and bought a home in the Valley. His home had a lovely redwood fence that was all the rage in San Fernando Valley in the forties. Ticker had come west with Dinah and on his first visit to the Songwriter's home remarked, "How could that guy sell you a house with an unpainted fence like that?" The alarmed songwriter immediately asked for advice and Ticker said, "Paint it!" and the beautiful redwood fence went undercover.

Next came the gophers. The Songwriter had no idea what these little creatures were who kept coming out of holes in his front yard, asked for help, and Ticker responded, "The only answer is raisins." The mystified songwriter was counseled to buy some raisins, sprinkle them in a circle around the hole where the gopher surfaced, arm himself with a baseball bat, and when the gopher emerged, blast him with the bat.

Gophers were crazy about raisins, Ticker advised, and would surface as soon as the sun went down. The poor Songwriter spent several fruitless evenings before he mentioned his activities to a more sympathetic soul and was told he'd been had.

Jerome Kern

PAUL

Before getting into records and radio as a conductor in Hollywood I did get a couple opportunities to do some arranging for motion pictures, and got to spend some time with two rather famous songwriters. The Bob Crosby band was hired to do some off-camera recording for *Holiday Inn* and I arranged most of Fred Astaire's dance numbers as well as duets with Astaire and Crosby and in doing so spent some unforgettable moments with Irving Berlin.

But the most interesting day was spent with Jerome Kern after I received a call to arrange a number for *Cover Girl*. Kern, Gene Kelly, Morris Stoloff and I were in a meeting where Stoloff was to tell us how the studio wanted to present one of Kern's ballads in the picture.

He started by saying they had decided to cut the verse. Kern immediately interrupted, loudly asking, "Why?" Stoloff tried to explain that the director felt the verse was unnecessary and again Kern almost shouted, "Why?" Stoloff started to get visibly nervous, made one more attempt, and again came this rasping question. With this Gene Kelly jumped up and said, "Oh, I forgot I'm due in wardrobe right away." And he darted out the door. Stoloff mumbled something about going to see the director, and there I was alone in the room with this wonderful little fellow who was then and still is my favorite composer.

He turned to me and said, "Young man, if you're ever going to get your way in this motion picture business you must learn to say 'Why?' in an extremely irritated tone of voice over and over again until you wear them down." Then he smiled as if we were co-conspirators and the verse stayed right where he wanted it.

The Capitol Records Story

PAUL

As the years have passed it has been pointed out to me that I am the lone survivor of the earliest creative Capitol group, and I thought it might be proper to set down my recollections of the start of what became a rather important record company.

My first connection with Johnny Mercer happened at Paramount Studios in 1942. The Bob Crosby band, for which I had been making arrangements, was suddenly (through Bing's suggestion) hired to make background tracks for *Holiday Inn*, and I found myself writing the charts for Fred Astaire's dances for this remarkable picture. Johnny Mercer was at the same time writing the songs for a picture called *Star Spangled Rhythm*, and our paths crossed.

Months later I received a phone call from John saying that he was about to make a record of a tune called "Strip Polka" for his newly formed company, Capitol Records. He wanted to know if I would like to make the arrangement and conduct the session. John had already made one record for Capitol, "They Didn't Believe Me," but only because the singer on the date wasn't able to handle the vocal and John had to step in.

Needless to say I was knocked out by "Strip Polka," and my arrangement (not all my doing) featured an announcement by Phil Silvers, piano by Jimmy Van Heusen, and a vocal trio of famous Hollywood group singers. I wrote some Guy Lombardo saxophone sounds that seemed to fit, and of course the record caused a lot of excitement. Shortly afterward Johnny asked me if I would like to be Capitol's musical director, and it took me about two seconds to answer in the affirmative. At that time Capitol consisted of one room in a building south of Sunset and Vine Street, and all the Capitol reference records fit in one lower desk drawer.

John's idea of record making was that of picking out a tune, making the arrangement and doing the session. Then if it didn't work out well, you either scrapped the idea or did it over. With him at the helm, very few things were ever done over.

When we had finished a session we were proud of, we brought the dubs to the room on Vine Street and listened to them at length and rather loudly at that. I can remember one day when Glenn Wallichs sat at the only desk in the room, while John and I impatiently turned on the playback turntable to hear our latest output.[1] Glenn was on the phone, and John said, "Glenn, come on and hang up—we want you to hear these sides." Glenn protested that he was on long distance trying to line up a distributor in Pittsburgh. John said, "Oh the hell with that, let's listen to the records!" John never did come to terms with the sales and other business aspects of the record business. He just wanted to make good records and put them out.

He put his group of artists together, and the first Capitol album was planned and recorded. It consisted of Johnny Mercer lyrics, recorded by John, Jo Stafford, The Pied Pipers (with Jo singing lead) and my orchestra—a group I put together with stalwarts like Eddie Miller and Matty Matlock and others from the Bob Crosby band.

Meanwhile, John allowed me to make my own album, *Music For Dreaming*, for which I was later either given the credit or the blame for creating Mood Music. We took the instrumentation of the dance band and added strings, and featured jazz solos by the many fine instrumentalists that had by now decided to make their home in California, and fortunately for me it was one of Capitol's first album hits.

John also signed Nat Cole, and his albums started one of the finest recording careers ever. Ella Mae Morse and Freddie Slack of course had a hit in "Cow Cow Boogie," and Margaret Whiting (with Billy Butterfield on trumpet) made "Moonlight in Vermont." Jo Stafford also did her first sessions in October 1943 and soon had her own album.

I'll never forget one session with Nat Cole. Buddy De Sylva's nephew, Dave Shelley took turns with us in producing sessions in the booth. Nat had a wonderful character who set-up his sessions and also acted as his bodyguard companion, although such a position was not really required in those days. We started the first tune—I was running things in the booth—when all of a sudden "Big John" (the set-up man) reached across me, hit the talk-back mic and said, "Hold it!" Nat said to me, "What's wrong?" I said, "I don't know. Big John said to hold it." Nat was of course furious and asked Big John what the problem was. Big John said, "I just didn't feel it!" Well, for a set-up man to stop a recording because he didn't feel it was really something. Nat yelled, "Who the hell does he think he is? George Bernard Shaw?" We all broke up and went back to work.

Once a week we'd have a meeting up in the lounge—we now had been able to move out of the one room. Glenn had an office, John had a little office next door, and the original back room was mine. A friend of mine from Dartmouth, Jim Conkling, came to California where, incidentally, I introduced him to his future wife, Donna King, on a blind date. He wanted to get into show business, so I brought him in to see Glenn. Glenn liked him right away and wanted Johnny Mercer to hire him, but knowing John he didn't want to make too big a pitch on his own in the creative field.

By this time Capitol and its artists had become well-known enough to attract the New York advertising agencies, and when Bob Hope took the summer off in 1943, the Pepsodent people hired Johnny Mercer to handle the summer replacement. Johnny asked Jo Stafford, Ella Mae Morse, The Pied Pipers, and the Paul Weston Orchestra to make up the show.[2] Since Jo found the solo singing and the Pied Piper work too much of a burden, June Hutton stepped in as lead singer for the Pipers. Johnny wrote the closing theme, "Dream," and much of the material, and the summer replacement was such a success that a few months later Chesterfield put the show on as the *Chesterfield Supper Club*.

To pursue the Capitol story—I took Jim Conkling over to meet Mercer at NBC. He gave Jim a sort of try-out mission—to go back to New York and report on a band that Mercer was thinking of hiring, and Jim wrote such a funny letter outlining the band's prospects (or in this case lack of them) that John hired him right away. So for the next several years, John, Jim and I were the Capitol artists and repertoire department and really enjoyed it. Dave Dexter had brought in Peggy Lee, Carlos Gastel had become involved with Stan Kenton and took over Nat Cole's management, and Capitol was on its way.

We still had a pretty artistic attitude towards the product. John never believed in releasing a lot of records, and of course had to change his thinking when the company began to be looked to for regular releases. I remember one release with three records on it: "Dream," "Candy," and "Ac-Cen-Tchu-Ate the Positive." They were three solid hits with Mercer either writing them or singing on them.

I remember sitting in John's living room writing down the melody and chords of "Dream" before we started using it as the Chesterfield closing theme. The second chord in the tune is important, and although I played every possible chord using the note of the melody, John never really heard what he wanted. We settled for the current harmonization. He would write the rhymed couplets that started the show on the stairway outside the control room just before we went on the air, and they were brilliant.

We always had a Friday afternoon meeting in the lounge, which was the only time we ever saw Buddy De Sylva, one of the three Capitol founders. Buddy was really pretty amazed at what his original contribution had wrought. He was very busy at Paramount Studios and had little to do with most of the Capitol activity.

I remember one conversation we had concerning John. He was disturbed, and rightly so, that John was spending a lot of his time with pretty untalented writers, who would call him up and get his commitment to work with them—John found it very difficult to refuse anyone. Buddy asked me what could be done about it and I replied, "Whoever shows up at John's house first thing in the morning has his commitment for the day." If someone comes along and says, "John, let's go up to Santa Barbara and snatch pocketbooks this morning," John would say, "fine" and off they'd go. I told Buddy this couldn't be corrected and of course it never was.

Some of the most interesting activity at Capitol took place before a Petrillo-called musician's strike.[3] We knew it was going to happen, and of course we tried to record as much product as we could so that we'd have records to release during the strike. Jim Conkling, John and I gathered all the songs we could lay our hands on and apportioned them among Capitol artists as best we could. Then we hastily made arrangements and scheduled round-the-clock recording sessions so we'd have plenty of releases.

By now Capitol had a country and western department with Lee Gillette and Cliffie Stone in charge, and the musicians gave them a most unusual problem. One of their stars was Merle Travis, a fine singer and a real free spirit. A few days before the strike, with a Merle Travis album half completed, a Los Angeles policeman made the mistake of pulling Merle over and suggested that Merle's motorcycle was going altogether too fast. Something in the policeman's attitude annoyed Merle, so he grabbed the policeman's ticket book, tore it in two and hit the policeman in the face with the pieces. Needless to say he was soon in jail, where Gillette found him when called in order to get the album finished. Gillette's efforts to spring him were laughed at and the story of the musician's strike had very little effect on the L.A.P.D. So Glenn Wallichs, Capitol's most solid citizen, went to the highest authority with his tale of the half-finished album. By now less than twenty-four hours remained before the strike, and Lee Gillette was very nervous indeed. Finally Glenn worked out a deal whereby Merle could come to the studio provided he remained handcuffed to a policeman throughout the session. Grasping at any straw offered, Gillette agreed, knowing that somehow he had to get the cuffs off so Merle could play his guitar.

Merle and the officer showed up right on time. Gillette then thought that a round of drinks might help the situation—sort of loosen things up. So several rounds followed and the officer was eventually talked into turning Merle loose long enough to play guitar, with the stipulation that the officer would stay in the studio with Merle in sight throughout the session. Things loosened up considerably and the album was completed.

Many years later Merle Travis told me the finish of the story. When the session was over the officer was so loaded that he drove Merle back to jail with the red light on and siren at full blast. Merle was as frightened as he's ever been in his life—and very pleased when they finally careened into the jail garage.

Jonathan and Darlene Edwards

PAUL

Through the years we've really enjoyed knowing and working with (or should I say being) Jonathan and Darlene. We're often asked how the silly adventure got started and as a matter of fact both of them appeared on the scene unprofessionally at first, along about 1955. Jonathan tended to present himself when things got a little quiet, or when people began taking themselves too seriously at a Hollywood party. At those times I would go to the piano and play what has now become Jonathan's larger-than-life style, which is that of the most horrible cocktail pianist at anytime, anywhere...wrong chords, wrong rhythm, wrong melody, a totally ridiculous musical effort.

Jeannie Martin, Dean's wife, used to ask me to go to the piano and "do that silly thing you do." I'd oblige, never realizing for a second that a conceiving of sorts was in the works. I was unaware I was courting an idea whose time was yet to come.

The birth—or the way it got started professionally, if you'll pardon the word—was at a Columbia Records convention in 1956, in Key West, Florida. We had had a full, heavy, tiring day of discussing the new product, meeting after meeting, bickering and bellowing in the traditional smoke filled rooms until the announcement, the most welcome announcement of a break for dinner was made.

We careened our way into the hotel dining room where this pianist was at his instrument, pouring out pathetic chords, twisting melodies into private traumas, courageously pounding away at his very personal and bewildering versions of popular songs. After a relentless and mutilating attack on the music of the day, he packed up and went home satisfied. I'm certain, that once again he felt that he had generously shared his talents, filling the ears of music-starved diners.

We were still at our table, sipping our brew, and the corner of my eye kept falling on the now empty, battle-scarred keyboard, memories of the mangy melodies floating in my head. It was an irresistible temptation. I made my way to the piano and very quietly started playing my Jonathan arrangement of "Stardust." I was doing it just for the fun of it, headily enjoying myself, when George Avakian and Irving Townsend came stumbling over to the piano, double up in laughter, and said, "Hey! You've got to make an album of that." It was the kind of remark one doesn't take seriously. I dismissed it with a resounding chord, was about to close the lid of the piano when they clutched at my hand and said, "We really mean it." They were each wearing their stern Columbia Records East Coast executive look, the one reserved for weighty decisions, and as the West Coast executive, a minority of one, I fought with, "What are you talking about? Who would buy that?" They wasted no words and a ringing, "Do it." was the final decree.

With the project of making a Jonathan album handed me, I came home and lightly set to work on some songs that had already been started, "Sunday, Monday, or Always," "Stardust," and things like that. These were songs I had semi-Jonathan type arrangements on, but I had never given any attention to the strict, formal idea of making twelve tunes. I panicked. I needed support and fortunately didn't have to go searching because my support emerged in the shape of my good wife. With a "presto," she was made part of what seemed to me to be a perilous, flighty project.

Jo jumped into the endeavor with reassurance, support and, strange for her, a very merry attitude. She christened herself Darlene and, in the words of the woman I call my good wife, here's how Darlene came to be…

Jo

During the years we were making records we used to get material from New York for me to consider recording. It was usually less than great, shall we say, but regardless of any lack of merit there would be orders-from-the-top; pressure put upon me to record some of these songs that were, to be absolutely truthful, terrible. Since the record company paid for everything, I had to be cooperative and a lot more cooperative than the artists who pay for their own sessions have to be these days. I was literally cornered and there was no escape from the fearful choices of songs handed me.

We would usually schedule four tunes and try to wind them up in three hours. If we finished fifteen or twenty minutes early with these duds that the musicians and I loathed, we'd spend the time left desecrating, musically crucifying the songs we had just recorded. The term for it is, "book style," and what it means is playing the melodies square and corny. I would sing out of tune and most importantly, I'd sing sharp, not flat. Sharp is worse than flat, much worse—sharp makes your teeth hurt. The fellows would play square, I'd sing sharp and we'd record the same songs, giving them the treatment we felt they deserved in the first place. It was in this disruptive environment that this bad lady singer was born, the lady who later took on the name of Darlene. Paul had already had the name of Jonathan Edwards so I became, naturally, darling Darlene Edwards.

PAUL

The interesting thing is that I didn't think of the name Jonathan Edwards. The name came from Columbia Records executive, George Avakian, who was a Yale graduate. George remembered that Jonathan Edwards had been a fundamentalist preacher and, at one time, the president of Yale University. To George's keen mind there was an analogy in that Roger Williams, who was then a famous pianist on the American pop music scene, was named after or had the same name as another Roger Williams, once a fundamentalist preacher in Rhode Island…to me, the melding of the two preachers and pianists was a brilliant stroke.

The time to record was approaching, I was in my addled state, and I appealed to Jo for help. I asked her to do four tunes, "book style." We selected four beauties: "You're Blasé," "Autumn in New York" (from that day Jo can't sing it correctly), "It's Magic," and "Cocktails for Two."

Jonathan played eight tunes including "Dizzy Fingers," "Nola," and several other winners. I hired my regular musicians to do the session with us. Nick Fatool, an outstanding drummer, laughed so hard at the end of one tune that he fell over his drums chortling and dropped his sticks on his drum set. That out-of-nowhere sound is still part of the original Jonathan and Darlene album.

In all honesty we thought we were just having fun and that nothing would ever happen with this album. Columbia, determined to issue it, put their best minds to work. So they enlisted some genius who came up with the album cover idea of having the pianist shown with a lovely girl at his side, playing with two right hands on the piano…you couldn't see anything of him, just his two right hands.

The album was then put out and certain disc jockeys tackled it within what seemed like seconds. Dick Whittinghill, one of the most prominent radio personalities in Los Angeles, and incidentally one of the original eight

Pied Pipers, was noted as somewhat of a talent scout. He went on the air and announced that he had found a new girl singer who was better than anyone he had ever heard. He played "It's Magic"—one of the tracks from the album—and immediately got an avalanche of phone calls saying, "We have trusted you all these years, all our lives. This woman is terrible, how can we ever believe in you again?" Some people told him they had to pull their cars off to the side of the freeway because they were afraid to drive while this woman was singing. It turned into a big scene around the country and no one knew or had the slightest idea who Jonathan and Darlene Edwards were or where they had come from. The jockeys were having a good time guessing, holding contests, seeking information about the "new two" when Time Magazine exposed us in an article titled "Two Right Hands."

Confidentially, we were both happy to be exposed. The gag built, the album became a decent seller and we were asked to do another. By this time Jonathan and Darlene began to take on their own personalities, they became dear and very real to us. Jonathan was a most defined man with "enthusiasm" as his watchword and artistic abandon was more important than hitting right notes. Darlene felt she should be unencumbered and allowed to take off into musical flights that might involve a few wrong notes here and there. The free-spirited couple felt they had deep integrity and did not welcome people pointing out their errors. It should be noted that after the first album one record buyer wrote Columbia, called attention to the two right hands, and asked for his money back because "there were some mistakes in the performance!"

Jo

It's interesting to note that to Paul and me Jonathan and Darlene became third person people. I found myself referring to Darlene as being real, substantial, an alter ego. When discussing wardrobe, for instance, I'd say, "No, no she wouldn't wear that. Not on your life!" Darlene may not be a terrific singer, but she's certainly not a clown. She would have fairly good taste, maybe a little flamboyant, maybe a little Helen Hokinson, maybe some flowered voile, but she would never be ridiculous.

Jonathan and Darlene had two great television experiences. The first one was on *The Garry Moore Show* in New York, which was produced by Joe Hamilton and had Carol Burnett as a regular on the program. The curious thing about Jonathan and Darlene is if you just go out and do them cold, twenty-five percent of the audience will react with "She may have sung a few notes out of tune, but she's good and he certainly can tickle those ivories." Garry Moore set the appearance up beautifully with his introduction:

> Jonathan is the epitome of all the bad cocktail pianists in the world, but he feels—and vehemently so—that slavish adherence to the chord patterns of the composer are not for him. He is much more of an artist than that and Darlene feels a few notes out of tune here and there are her prerogative and her skill demands such liberties.

That summation of his introduction was that Jonathan and Darlene were bad. When we finished doing our number on *The Garry Moore Show* the applause was so loud and so sustained that Garry couldn't make his next announcement and they were forced to "go to black" and put on a commercial. That was a kick for us—it was the first time we'd ever done the act in public.

PAUL

Our biggest thrill—great fun for Jo and myself—was a guest shot on *The Jack Benny Show*, with the only guest stars being Ed Wynn and us. Benny heard the album, loved it and invited us to do his show. As Jo Stafford and Paul Weston we might have been asked to do a guest spot, but it took Jonathan and Darlene to get written into the entire show. Jack had this awful song he'd written, which he used throughout his radio and television career called, "When You Say I Beg Your Pardon, Then I'll Come Back to You." It was a dreary song and Jack was always running around, trying to get people to record it, but no one would touch it with a ten-foot pole. He was politely brushed off on all counts.

The idea of his television show was that he was thrilled with the idea that Jo Stafford might possibly record his song. We were sitting in Jack's "living room" waiting for him to come home and Ed Wynn said, "You're not going to record that terrible song, are you?" Jo told Ed that Jack had asked her to and she was in a spot, she didn't know what to do, how to wiggle out of it. Ed Wynn suggested that we do it as Jonathan and Darlene, "tear it to pieces and be so horrible that Jack will realize he really doesn't want you to do it, and he won't be pestering you anymore." We agreed it was a great suggestion when Jack appeared at the door, walked in, threw down a sheath of paper and said, "I have an arrangement here for a thirty-five piece orchestra on 'When You Say I Beg Your Pardon,

Then I'll Come Back to You.'" After a stunned pause, Ed Wynn asked Jack to first listen to our ideas about his song, to hear us do it. Jack said fine, went to the couch and sat down. I went over to the piano, gave a terrifying Jonathan arpeggio and Jo started singing the song as only Darlene can sing—awful! Jack sat listening, never moving throughout the song, and we finished, thinking we were secure that he would never want to hear from us again, when he turned with that familiar profile look and said, "Wonderful!" He wanted that song recorded so badly he'd even accept a Jonathan and Darlene Edwards perversion. Ed Wynn fell on the floor, we did too, and that night was for us, never to be forgotten.

A sidelight story to the Benny show was the surprising reaction of our son, Timothy, who was then about four-years-old and a great fan and truly devoted admirer of Jack Benny. We took him to the show and sat him with his Aunt Tina in the audience, thinking it would be a special treat for him. After the show, when it came time to go home, we fetched him, but he adamantly refused to get into the car with us. His Aunt had to take him home and for the next twenty-four hours he refused to speak to us because he felt we had played a joke on Mr. Benny. In his own childlike way he found it intolerable that we pulled such a "naughty trick."

It's been over twenty-one years since Jonathan and Darlene were first heard, but the fan mail still goes on. The albums are still selling and they still are the cause of strange incidents.

Jo

It was about a year ago that Paul and I were in Hawaii, having dinner at a restaurant and a perfect stranger, a lady, came up to the table and said, "I want to thank Jonathan and Darlene Edwards for saving me from a bad marriage," which was a pretty strong opening statement from a total stranger. We asked her to tell us about it and she said,

> Well, I've always been crazy about Jonathan and Darlene. I was about to marry this man and I wanted to share some of my favorite things with him. Without saying a word I put the album on one day and eagerly watched for his reaction, hoping it would be as enthusiastic as mine. I kept waiting for him to laugh and when he didn't my impatience got me and said, "Isn't that funny?" He sullenly said, "What's so funny about that?" My son from a previous marriage said to me later, "Mom, you can't marry that guy. He hasn't any sense of

humor." I didn't marry him and it was the greatest thing that ever happened to me. I've always been grateful to Jonathan and Darlene for helping me avoid a bad marriage.

Jonathan and Darlene were also a boon to getting rid of guests at an over-extended cocktail party. We had a letter from a man in New York who used the record regularly when guests overstayed their welcome at his parties. When the booze began to flow uncorked and drunken drama loomed, he would sneak over to the phonograph and put the album on. Within minutes the revelers, hearing the sound, would be convinced they were a lot drunker than they thought and make a hasty departure. He wrote, "Jonathan and Darlene cleared the apartment better than Flit."[4]

PAUL

A good friend of Jo's and mine is Norman Luboff, the director of the Norman Luboff choir, with whom we've recorded many times. Norman brought the album with him to a party one evening and at the party was a woman whose brother, an unsuccessful tenor, was visiting her from New York. Being an unsuccessful tenor from wherever is tough, but an unsuccessful tenor from New York means you're really unsuccessful. Without any fanfare, Norman put on the album and Darlene sang one chorus of "It's Magic" and this woman turned on her brother with the fury of a tigress and said, "If she can get a recording contract, why can't you?" Norman, completely unbelieving, went over to the player, got his record and silently walked out the door.

Jonathan and Darlene were created, in their own individual images, out of the clay of discord and disharmony. They received their highest honor with a Grammy Award in 1960—given by the National Academy of Recording Arts and Sciences. They were a little confused at receiving the award in the category Best Comedy Album–Musical, but they accepted it nonetheless.

Even at this moment they have plans for their tomorrow. They are lustily working on a new album, *Darlene Remembers Duke, Jonathan Plays Basie*, which will be eventually released.[5] Without their total dedication and musical integrity there would never have been the adulation, the lauding and the fawning.

The Ducks Are Drowning

PAUL

It was not the worst of times, nor the best of times for those of us who worked in Hollywood in the period before the advent of videotape. It was the time of live television, which could only be described as exciting, unpredictable, and often downright perilous.

There was no such thing as a second chance. Vaudeville performers took months to work up a routine and then used it for years. In the theater and in opera the material was engraved in the memories of the actors and singers. In radio one read from a script, with emergencies handled out of sight of the audience. And, of course, in the movies the same scene was done over and over until everyone was patent leather perfect.

But live television was something else altogether. There was never enough time to rehearse, and once you went on the air there was no turning back. Cuts and changes were made right up until show time, and mistakes were viewed by millions of people. The odds were stacked against a smooth, precise performance and the possibility of disaster was always in the mind of everyone concerned. Videotape arrived in the late fifties with its comforting cop-out of "take two!" And that was the end of totally live television, but it was sure fun while it lasted.

I'll never forget one incident...Jo and I were doing a Chevrolet show—a very *live* Chevy show—under the aegis of the great, famous, infamous, Alan Handley, who throughout the fifties was the most sought after producer of television variety shows. Alan had so little interest in music that he usually had it turned off in the control booth while he concerned himself with the picture, and when I would ask how the music sounded the answer was always "I don't know—that's your problem!"

It was probably his indifference to all things musical that led him to the situation where Jo was to lie on her back and sing "Almost Like Being In Love."

Now singing sitting down is pretty dumb, and singing lying on one's back is just plain stupid. Alan had Jo reclining on a mossy bank, delicate indications of spring abounded, and to her immediate left was a six-foot water wheel. The plan was for the wheel to rotate majestically and scoop droplets of water out of a lovely little pond, on the tranquil surface of which a group of smallish ducks was to paddle happily about. Meanwhile Jo was to sing gaily about what a rare mood she was in and what a day it had been. Her comments concerning her recumbent position were mostly unprintable. So while he was a very good producer, Alan Handley was also very autocratic, and imperiously waved off any dissent.

My orchestra was about thirty feet away from this pastoral scene and I was equipped with a headset, that wonderful contraption that splits a conductor's head in two. You listen to the singer in one ear and the other ear is the helpless victim of all the screaming confusion going on in the control booth, plus reciprocal exchanges between the director, floor managers, cameramen and audio boom operators. Often this byplay is much funnier than the show itself.

We started calmly enough with the premise that the water wheel would be an important part of the number—certainly in Alan's mind considerably more important than the music. The only problem was that we hadn't had sufficient rehearsal time to test everything, and on the air we went at nine in the evening Eastern Standard Time taking our best shot because it was the only one we were ever going to get. There was no "take two."

None of us had any idea of what might happen when the water wheel started revolving. Needless to say, if it had gone round at a gentle pace things would have been fine. Unfortunately, a nervous assistant floor manager had been put in charge of controlling the wheel's motion, and the pressure just got to him. Its pace soon turned from majestic to frantic, and disaster loomed.

We were about eight bars into the song, with Jo singing beautifully into my right ear, when my left ear was assaulted by a frenzied message from floor to control booth in what should have been a stage whisper, but really was a muffled scream, "The ducks are drowning! The ducks are drowning!!"

My eyes darted over to Jo's left, and sure enough the water wheel was revolving at a merry clip, sucking in the ducks as they swam ever more frantically trying to avoid their fate. Meanwhile the poor stage manager was scooping them out of the wheel and tossing them back into the pond, at the same time screaming at his assistant in another would-be stage whisper to "Slow down the goddamn wheel!"

The barely suppressed hysteria to her left was certainly audible to Jo, but as she lay on her back all she could see was directly above her, and there was nothing happening up there. But she knew one thing—this was live television, you had to keep singing—there was no turning back. So she stayed right there on her grassy bank and forged ahead with her happy lyrics.

Now I have always believed that if a performer collapsed on stage during one of his shows Alan Handley would have calmly shot the scenery for a few seconds and then turned his cameras back on center stage, expecting that his stage crew would have immediately grabbed a replacement and lugged off the offending artist. He certainly wasn't going to be too upset over a few drowning ducks. So he just ordered, "Fix it!" and kept his cameras on good old uncomfortable Jo until his crew got things under control. The wheel slowed down, the wounded ducks were removed, and the survivors paddled about the pool. Their experience had scared them and they darted rather nervously, staying well clear of the water wheel, but they were considered photographable, and the number finished as it had begun.

I've heard some crazy things in my headset over the years, but never anything more pathetic than the cry, "The ducks are drowning!" Ducks don't drown—they weren't drowning—they were being endangered by a very nervous assistant floor manager. But that was live television—exciting, unpredictable and, for the ducks, downright perilous. We wouldn't have missed it for the world.

P.W.'s score for the closing theme to Johnny Mercer's Music Shop.

A Wetstein arrangement of "Memphis Blues" used on Johnny Mercer's Music Shop. Paul adopted the name Weston starting with the premier of this show (dated August 11, 1943).

Tommy Dorsey Orchestra (1941).

Jonathan and Darlene Edwards make an appearance on the Merv Griffin Show.

Correspondence

350 W 57th St., Apt #5J
New York, New York
*New York addresses are always
more impressive than suburban ones.*

[ca. March 1, 1945][6]

Dear Honey-Dreamboat,[7]
    We have one too. It's a Royal (the portable type) [and] we carry it with us no matter where we may go. It isn't the silent kind though. This one makes noise. Get me out of here!
    Well things aren't as bad as when you were here—the hours I mean. It's only midnight and here I am home zizzing out a letter to you—on the noisy portable type. Jimmy and Dario wish they were dead and I'm as happy as a bee in a bonnet.[8] Which is about as happy as I can get in the present set-up. It's really scads better though.
    I wish we had been in this apartment when you were here. It has a piano and we could have tried out that Debussy idea you thought about. It's really a very nice place but we both hate it. I can't get over the feeling that I'm living in someone else's house. The natural inclination at this point is to say, "well, wadhead you are." But nevertheless I wish we had never moved out of the Gotham. It's furnished very nicely, but the bed has got to have a story behind it. Ethel must have had it made to order. You could never just go in and say, "Sam, let me see what you have in beds" and come up with this atrocity. It's one of those large jobs. And whatever took the place of springs? My muscles were actually sore after my first night on the lame thing. Even in my sleep I have a sort of "hang on for dear life" feeling. This is due to the large hump in the middle of the mattress. Maybe this type bed

makes for a better embouchure on the Hammond organ. There's got to be a reason—and "by gawd" I intend to discover it.

I'm gonna have a spread in *Look* magazine in four or five weeks. I gave you and the Prez a good deal of credit for my present fame and fortune.[9] Hope they use it. The article will probably read something like this when they finish though, "This is a picture of Jo Stafford, she sings."

I'm pleased no end with the news of my next release—that's the finest kind.

What the devil is John Hud doing in Hollywood?[10] I swear, I'd be getting a little embarrassed with these farewells. The last I heard he was practically ready to go over the big pond. It's gonna be over *over there* before he gets to Fresno. Natch, I'd be forever thankful to heaven if he never went anyplace more dangerous than the tropics.[11] But at this point I'm a little puzzled. He owes me a letter so I suppose I'll find out about stuff.

This curfew has really got this town on its ears.[12] I suppose it's quite tragic for the cafe owners. The Copa has completely closed down. Dario might as well if business doesn't pick up. You could have shot deer in the place last night. It was slightly better tonight, but not much. Here's one for the books. The night after the ruling went in they gave everybody in the place two weeks' notice but me. When I found out they were handing them out I started hanging around Jimmy and Dario, trying not to look too eager—and nothing happened. In fact they came around the next day and wanted me to stay on for an extra month. What am I gonna use for accompaniment, bones? The only thing this curfew proves to me is a protestant's prayers are answered sometimes. And if I'm fired I may join the church.

I'm doing a great shot on the *Philco Show* next Sunday. You probably know about it. They were gonna ask you for the score on "[I] Promise You."[13] I thought as long as I was singing the song I might as well do the record arrangement. I hope it was all right to ask for it. You and "Merc" are such strange characters though.[14] One never knows how you're gonna feel about things. Speaking about the Philco show, thanks heaps to both you and the Colonel for letting me not know he was on it last Sunday. I found out on Monday through vague channels. Guess I don't rate in the backroom anymore. All I can say is, it doesn't take you guys long to ease a person out. I suppose all you can hear around there now is, Ella Mae, Ella Mae, Ella Mae![15] The pox on both of you. I just finished reading *Forever Amber*—and that's a saying they use.

I was interviewed tonight on a record show, one of the records they used was "Candy"—and I felt real sad when I heard it. Thinking of the fun I was having about the time we made it. Seems I don't have any fun times anymore. No kiddin', I haven't had a good time since you left. I've met a lot of people, but they're all sort of the "Where ever is that?" sort—and they gave me a pain in the you know where. I don't know anyone that I can be the real me with. I'm getting sulky and sullen too. The other day I said, "to hell with the flag." That isn't the proper attitude, do you think? I don't think I'll ever get back. Maybe I'll become a confirmed New Yorker and eat raw oysters and clams, call the mayor "the little flower," and all that stuff—and as an afterthought, kill myself.

I think Ella Mae should record "Leave Us Go Dancing" in boogie woogie time—that's an eight-to-the-bar beat. With whatever else you can find thrown in, and a running bass, it just keeps going like mad all the time. The arrangement should be black as hell, especially if she's still engaged to Louis Prima.[16]

I'm glad the records you made were good. A completely successful record date in New York should make you more insufferable than ever concerning your talent. Seeing as how they're fairly rare, however, I'm very happy for you. I suppose you've told John all sorts of lies about that girl hurting that silly old E flat, "pish and tosh," that's all I have to say on that matter.[17]

I still have the tail end of that cold. How can you get rid of them here? It has been raining like mad and the weather is still cold. Chris also has a beauty and Pauline is worse off than both of us.[18] She's in bed, eh law.[19]

Please don't harm the *hat*. The first time I see you again I want you to have it on. It's one of my fondest memories in this dark period of my life. You may hide it if you like, for the present, but please don't destroy it. If you do, all is off between us.

The neuritis in my right shoulder is killin' me from pounding this thing. So I'd better stop. Please write soon. Your last letter is getting all dirty and wrinkled from re-readings. Give everyone my love and envy—'specially you.

Love,
Baby

[April 13, 1945][20]
Jo-Ann Baby,

This is perfectly ridiculous—me writing you after receiving naught but a state post card. And I am sustained only by the firm conviction that somewhere between here and New York City is a war missive from you to me—already dispatched on its merry way. If this hope is groundless you may consider our association completely at an end. My sentiments in this matter are sharply associated by the prevalent rumors: I. New York City—You and Mike Nidorf are a distinct item (understand it's in all the columns).[21] II. There is a somewhat garbled report circulated here by several—including Dinah Shore—that you and I are "going together."

Now it's obviously impossible for a man of my position to put up with the above transcontinental mix-up. "Baby. Is you is or is you ain't [my baby]!?" My immediate impulse is to call Louella Parsons and announce that we have *pfffit* and that you are carrying the torch of all time. I plan to do that if I haven't heard from you by Saturday or if I hear any more ridiculous reports from my New York office concerning you and the poor man's Ken Dolan.[22] Let's hear from you sweetie—and pronto (a Mexican word meaning yesterday).

It seems pretty hokey writing any jazz after the terrible news we all heard today. We had just finished dress rehearsal for Burns when I heard the news. And we were all at the office at the time. Just seemed unbelievable for a long time. I hope you heard Orson Welles from Hollywood—pretty impressive. I really think he's a great man. I know you felt as strongly about Roosevelt as I did and the whole thing is pretty shocking.[23]

I got a wire from Mildred saying the arrangements arrived OK.[24] Hope they sound all right and I'm sure you'll be a big hit. Had dinner at Bing's again Sunday and he said you'd be a "swosh" at the Paramount.[25] Also told someone after he heard your record of "I Promise You" and "Long Way Home" he didn't feel like trying to sing them anymore. That should make you pretty happy. *Write soon*, give my best to the character and take care.

Love,
Paul

[April 15, 1945][26]
Dear Baby Doll Honey Sweetie,

    I'm still a bit confused after talking all the way to New York City twice in one day. But it sure *were* nice to hear your sleepy voice again. I suppose you know about Mike calling me and I must confess I'm a little mystified by the whole thing. He was sort of indefinite about it all. And I don't know how much of the whole thing you know or whether I'm supposed to talk with you about it but I am—so there. And I don't know what the hell the whole thing's about in the first place. And now I'm happy because you're as confused as I am.

    He seemed to be talking about the five-a-week Chesterfield show, but I couldn't quite figure where you figured. Whether you were to be on every day or whether [Perry] Como was to be on some—or what. At any rate I told him I might come back there for thirteen weeks *if* it would move to the coast after that; but that I was only interested *if* it was your show and that I didn't want to come back there on the same basis as [Ted] Steele and make a lot of arrangements for jerky people I don't want to have anything to do with.[27] I could go for a month or two of it if it were what we've been looking for. And if we could be certain that it would move out here. Mike finally wound up asking me if I could recommend anyone back there to do the job, but I couldn't think of anyone offhand. I told him the record company was the important thing in the long run for me and I really would prefer to stay here. He swore me to complete secrecy on the whole affair, which I am breaking only to let you in on the situation. So don't say anything about it unless he brings it up. I wouldn't be interested in coming back at all if it isn't [going] to be your own show. So if he has any ideas along other lines it might be well if you could discourage them. Tell him we have a pact, that we stabbed our arms and mixed our blood and have sworn to be eternal radio companions. Tell him anything you think of, but let's not get stuck back there forever, shall we. Hey baby?

    Enough for stupid business. I wish I had you here so I could beat you over the head every hour on the half-hour for three days for taking so many sleeping pills. No wonder you passed out. I guess I would have given two tickets to *Hobby Lobby*, a Clark Bar, and an autographed picture of Gil Johnson just to see you in that wheelchair.[28] Boy I almost fall down laughing just to think about it. I must know the exact route you travelled so I can imagine every foot of it. Was there a crowd of small boys and a nurse or two with smelling salts? It seems so unfair that I should have to miss it.

Mike was pretty hysterical about what a big hit you are in the theater—talking and all. But I suppose it's true and the next thing I know you'll probably be the M.C. in a cabaret—cracking wise and killing people. I must admit I had no fears whatsoever about theaters because the record buying people are in your pocket. By the way, I have a little exclusive Capitol news. Your record of "[A] Friend of Yours" and "Sunny Side" is coming out a month earlier—namely May 25. And "Conversation" won't be out for a while.[29] I also heard that Dinah is making "Sunny Side." So perhaps we'll have to carve her again. I hope word doesn't get around about your record, because then she might get scared and change her mind about making it.

There has been very little excitement since you done departed. Gordon's radio work has been pretty heavy, but I must admit I sure like it.[30] Seems wonderful to be back on the wireless, even with Helen Forrest and that greatest of all specialty singers, Shirley Ross. Hey come on Jo, get a nice show back here with a band as big as *Auto-Lite* so we can have some fun.[31] John seems to have given up all desire to ever get with it again. He was real dragged Thursday—maybe partly because of the President. Everyone here has been pretty brought down for three days. A lot of dopey people all of a sudden realizing that Roosevelt was a pretty great person.

I sure do envy you, Katherine Cornell must have been wonderful.[32] We have Toscanini Thursday night. [He] has everyone here quite excited—although he's playing some sort of junky stuff. Hey by the way, if you have a machine there—or if Pauline and "Ruck" have one—get Victor Young's album from *For Whom the Bell Tolls*.[33] I heard it on the air last night and the Spanish guitar work is terrific. I'm going to try to get it tomorrow.

I guess your second letter will arrive tomorrow and I could wait and make some extremely clever comments on the contents. But that would mean that this letter would reach you a day later and that is unthinkable. Write soon and keep assuring me of your undying devotion. New York, N.Y. is a tricky place—as who needs to tell you—and for all I know some smart talking gigolo may even now have you in his nefarious clutches. And watching the columns I am. Chris' card from Chicago was a positive scream and I loved the picture of the fish.[34] Sorry to have made so much of the letter on business subjects, but I do want to make it clear to Mike that I'm really not interested in coming back there for any show that isn't your own. Perry Como is a nice lad, but he doesn't "chill me" too much. And it's real nice out here. Hurry back.

Love,
Phineas

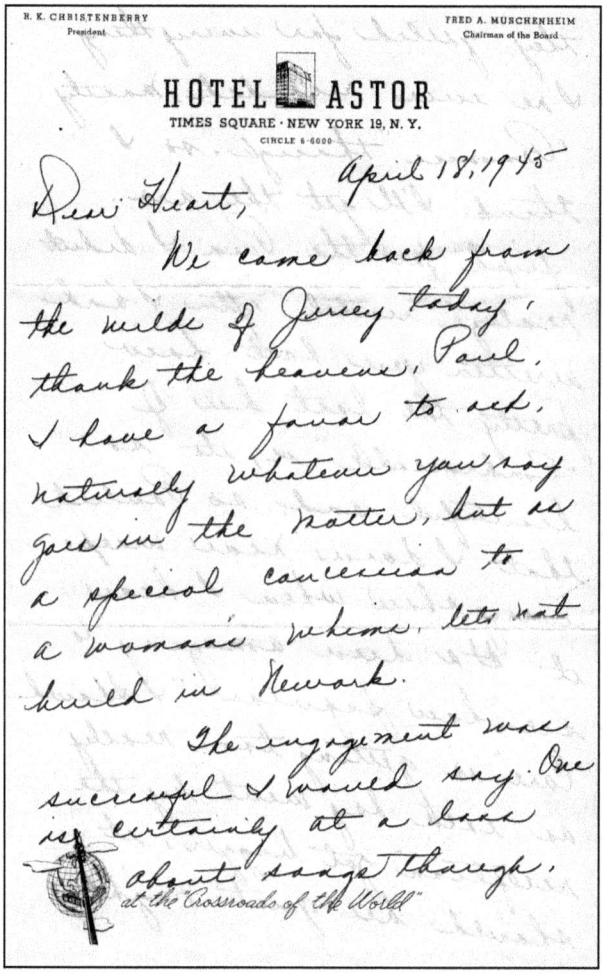

Jo Stafford letter dated April 18, 1945. Courtesy of Amy Weston.

Hotel Astor
Times Square
New York 19, NY

April 18, 1945
Dear Heart,
    We came back from the wilds of Jersey today—thank the heavens. Paul, I have a favor to ask. Naturally whatever you say goes in the matter. But as a special concession to a woman's whims—let's not build in Newark.

The engagement was successful I would say. One is certainly at a loss about songs though. They yelled for everything I ever recorded. Mostly "Promise" though.[35] So I think I'll get the arrangement fixed for the Paramount. I didn't realize until after I had written you last how pretty the last bar of "Embraceable You" is. It's so beautiful and so Paulish that I darn near weep every show when I hear it.[36] It's keen amazing to see how popular "I Should Care" is getting too.[37] Really as each day went by the reception got bigger. It should be just right in the Paramount.

I was pretty sure of your reaction on the deal Mike phoned about. He told me about it. However, I guess he wasn't supposed to. It's a big secret. Why don't these people stop? Everything has to be hush-hush. Wonder if they've told Como he's on the air yet? I think the whole deal amounts to this. They aren't satisfied with Ted Steele—who is? besides Mary Ashworth[38]—and they think you're the man for the job. As for me, Chesterfield would like me to work for them, but they don't know the spot as yet. The idea was for Como to be on [at] three and me on [at] two. Personally, I'm not too thrilled with it unless you were on. And I can understand your attitude perfectly. I'd do the same thing. All the while Rockwell is still working on the three-a-week CBS show for you and me[39]—which is much better I think. I've been receiving pep talks all week long from George Evans about how if I want to I can be the biggest thing in female singers in a year if I chance to be[40]—and will really work at it. Mike seems to think the Paramount will be a very good thing towards that end. I gather I'm gonna really get a workout in the coming weeks. Everything practically from kissing the Mayor to the key of the city presentation. Mike says create enough talk about yourself, get famous enough and you can have a radio program coming from Iwo Jima if you want it—with Hitler as guest star. So I've decided to do everything they throw at me. Work like I've never worked before and see what happens. I have every confidence that you and I will wind up where we want to. It may take a while that's all. Be patient love. Jeepers, so much business. I've been talking shop so much this week I can't stop.

I'm very thrilled about having a release in May. That's pretty hot, huh? I love Capitol, and I love everybody at Capitol—even [Lee] Gillette I guess. Well …

Listen Paul, I have been going places with Mike. But I certainly don't know how such [a story] as that got in Winchell's.[41] And what's more I don't imagine you've been sitting at home reading the Bible every night. You didn't say anything about me being your "baby" before I left. And what's more you can go on for years playing "Ring Around the Rosie," [or] circling Mulberry bushes. I don't even know if Mulberries are any good. I don't even know what Emily Post says.[42] But where I come from boys assert themselves, not girls. I knew I shouldn't have driven out to your house that night. Here we go around the bushes again.

I saw *Harvey* and thought it was wonderful.[43] Still not as good as *Apley* though.[44] Fay was marvelous.[45] He's always been a favorite of mine.

We had an act on with us at the Adams that it's a pity you missed. Chris committed the whole thing for you though and goes on stage at our next meeting.[46]

It is now four o'clock in the a.m. and the "last of the red-hot mamas" has to be at Victor tomorrow at ten to make records for the Army. So she'd better go to bed. It should be fun. I'm having a small orchestra with such beat-up players as [Billy] Butterfield, [Hank] D'Amico, Lou McGarity, [Carl] Kress, and [George] Wettling. No arrangement. We're just doing some oldies but goodies. Ouch! And also some blues. Wish you could be there, my darlin'.

Write soon and please don't marry that Whiting girl.[47] Pat Johnson may give in any day. Have a Mulberry. I love you, I do.

Chloe

This is the next night.

I decided not to mail my letter 'til after the record date, so I could tell you if it was good. I haven't got a good writing pen either—[this pen is] compliments of the Astor Hotel.

Gee doll, I wish you could have been there this morning. We had a marvelous date. I sang jazz and I think I did pretty good. George Simon was in charge.[48] I made: "Am I Blue," "Lonesome Road," "Blue Moon," "I'm Comin' Virginia," "Baby Won't You Please Come Home," and some blues. The players were just wonderful. George is having some copies of the records made and as I get them I'll send them on to you so you can hear them. Take good care of 'em, as they're all I'll be able to get. You can keep care of them until I get home. I'm a little upset about the blues number. After I got home I realized the lyrics are sorta suggestive. I didn't even think about it. At the time I was having so much fun, but Chris and Pauline looked slightly upset when I repeated the words. They'll only be played overseas though and it was fun to sing 'em. I hope you like the records. I think Billy was just wonderful. Also McGarity—well everyone was. I don't know how soon I'll get copies. I'll send them as soon as I get them though. Be sure and be careful of them.

Honey face, we've had the *Bell Tolls* album at home all the time.[49] That's where I first heard the Spanish music we've talked about. I thought you knew we had it. Tell me about the Toscanini concert—hope it was good. Also, hope you had some babe with you that doesn't know a quarter note from a kidney bean—so you'll hate her. 'Scuse this pen. I can hardly write with it.

Write soon and leave me know,
Baby

P.S. Give my love to Annie O'Grady and her "steady."[50]

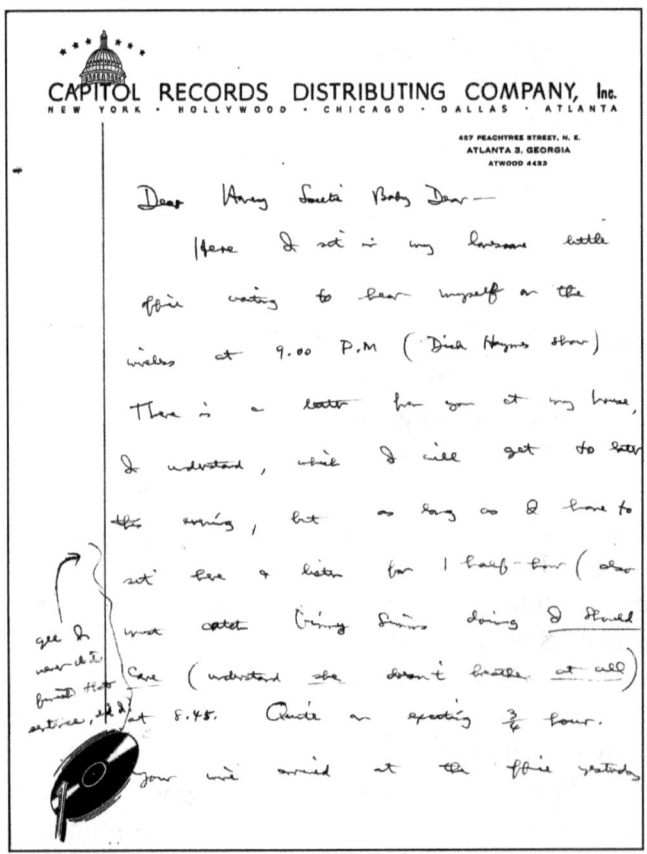

Letter from Paul Weston postmarked April 19, 1945. Courtesy of Tim Weston.

[April 19, 1945][51]
Dear Honey Sweetie Baby Dear,

Here I sit in my lonesome little office waiting to hear myself on the wireless at 9:00 p.m. ([I'm on the] *Dick Haymes Show*). There is a letter from you at my house I understand—which I will get to later this evening. But as long as I have to sit here and listen for one half hour, [I] also must catch Ginny Simms doing "I Should Care" at 8:45. [I] understand she doesn't breathe *at all*. Quite an exciting three-quarter hour.

Your wire arrived at the office yesterday. And when I called in from Brentwood for messages, this stoop Janet on the front desk says, "Well, you had a wire, but it seemed *quite personal*. So I didn't read *all* of it." Just shows what that signature "Baby" can do.

Was sorting over some old records the other night and almost fell over when I discovered a record of "Stop, Look and Listen" by the Camel Chorus (Jo Stafford singing at the age of 19).[52] Really pretty hot—your voice sounded quite youthful. Gee how old can we all get? I'll keep the record in waxed paper 'til you get back.

Got a rude shock today. Eddie Cantor is the guest on *Auto-Lite* next week. I'm going to send an S.O.S. wire to Gordon to get back here in a hurry.

Had a laugh from Shaky today. He and Herman were up in front of the Tropics [and were] mad as hell because John had kept them waiting to see him for forty-five minutes.[53] They finally walked out. They have a new excuse for not selling the show; Roosevelt's death has caused all advertiser's to cut down on budgets. Didn't take long for that reaction to make itself felt?

Told John you were on Ford [this] Sunday and he raised his eyebrows as to your classy company on that show. Are you the poor man's Vivian Della Chiesa?[54]

Am now at home and have read your letter. At least I'm glad you're good and healthy. Of course I'm only feeling fair. My little eyes hurt. I'm tired and sometimes I think I have a tapeworm and an inferiority complex. What do you think? We're doing the Lois Butler date Friday night and I'll try to do the "There's No You" arrangement next week.[55] Wire me if you find you don't need it. It sure is a hell of a fine record and is being played night and day out here.

I guess you really got something baby. The Orpheum Theatre called the Capitol office— wanted you in there and wanted to know your manager. Jim told them Mike was the man.[56] Jim's going East in a couple of weeks. See you crashed Winchell's column. No comment. I'm sure you can't read a word of this and I'll type the next letter. Let's hear from you baby. You write real entertaining parchments. You must have a swell personality.

Love,
Renbrew

Hotel Astor
Times Square
New York 19, NY

April 22, 1945
Dear Love-life,

Here I sit in my spacious suite at the Astor Hotel, wishing I was in Fresno. There's a sad girl in New York tonight—a sad girl. If I had Henry Ford's program [with] all his cars—including the Continental—and the old boy was standing in front of me himself, I'd have a few choice words to say at him as to what he could do with the whole lot.[57] As you can see I'm definitely not in my schoolteacher mood this evening. Excuse me, please. I hope you received my wire giving you full instructions as to what to do on Sunday. Anything but listen to that 1910 overture—"Old Fashioned Garden" indeed. I'll old fashion somebody's garden if I ever get caught in anything like that again. I was supposed to be on again next Sunday, but I threatened to kill myself. I wouldn't sing with that music if it meant running off with Charlie Wick for survival.[58] [I don't know] if you were unfortunate enough to have heard it. How about the one chord they used in "[The] Boy Next Door"?[59] At the end where the lyrics are "I can't ignore him, cause I just adore *him*," On the word him, they actually used the dominant 7th. I swear I didn't dare eat anything before the broadcast. Or you know what I'd have done at that particular period in musical history.

I almost called you when I returned from rehearsal. I was so brought down. Maybe it wouldn't have been so bad if I'd been singing a song I didn't like so much. But our dearly loved "Boy Next Door"? Please forgive me baby. I'm glad I didn't call you now. I'd have probably wept it up and made a scene and gotten you thoroughly disgusted. But I just kept thinking if I could just hear your voice and you could explain that in spite of Henry Ford the future of music has something. Oh well, you live and learn. Or I just live and become more convinced that there are two styles of music: with and without Weston. By now you've gathered my opinion of the latter. I refuse to waste any more ink on a subject that couldn't possibly interest you as much as me. I'm just upset, that's all.

Paul, I didn't know those office girls opened your wires or I wouldn't have put "Baby" on it. Hope you weren't upset or anything.

Hope Cantor will be loads of fun. You have Cantor, I have the *Ford Show*, and Germany has Hitler.

Hey, how was the Lois Butler thing? Gee I wish I could have heard it. Tell me all about it. Did you do good and did you like [the] music that night?

I got a letter from John Hud. In his absence he knew nothing about my change of agents. So he said he'd read in Winchell's column about me and my agent and asked me if I didn't think "Bullets" was a little small for me.[60] I darn near fell over laughing.

"Ruck" and Pauline have a new home. They can't move until June 15 however. I haven't seen it but they say it's out of the world. It's a penthouse at the Essex House—all privately owned furniture. It was Joanie Tapp's place. They bought furniture and all. Also a three sided terrace which will be nice this summer. Ruck will undoubtedly assume a Jimmy Walkerish air and take up spats.[61] I was gonna say and a homburg hat. But it suddenly came to me that he has owned one of those for some time. Mrs. Tapps is leaving everything except her sheets—even down to the ash trays.

Called home tonight and had quite a lengthy conversation with Christopher.[62] Once I can get him over ish-ish-ish like my car he talks furiously on varied subjects. All of which must sound like a Jap spy to the operator if she tuned in. He's the character of all time—and about my favorite.

Listen "Flintheart," how about sending me a bill for your frenzied efforts on my behalf when I was last seen on the Pacific Coast.[63] Remember how tired your poor little eyes got?

I only sat down to write a couple of pages and this takes place. The neuritis in my right shoulder is paining me from all this scribbling.

Write soon and assure me that next to several blondes, including Pat Johnson, you think I'm sweet.

Your ever-loving

Conductor part for P.W.'s arrangement.

[April 27, 1945][64]
Jo Anne My Sweet,

I'm at the office waiting for our Jerry Colonna record date to happen—[which] will undoubtedly be very dull—and still haven't been out home since I talked to you Wednesday night. John and I almost called you last night. I may call you tonight when he gets back from seeing De Sylva. Nothing much new has happened except that I'm going to Palm Springs tomorrow for three days. Figure I'll take my folks down there to see the place. It will probably be too hot after this weekend. Besides I deserve a rest after all the radio show and record dates. John surprised me by agreeing with me yesterday that the Ford and Prudential programs were great things for you—so there. You've been hanging around Leonard Feather too much, Jack—and your boots are too tight. Or maybe John and I are real old all of a sudden.

I am extremely happy about the reaction to your latest recording. I was scared of "Out of This World" and "There's No You," but it looks as if all will be very fine. I still don't know if we're smart or lucky. If you really want an arrangement for the Paramount or the latter tune—wire me here. I'll do it first thing next week.

Please honey send the record with the risqué lyrics, because I'm going to have it dubbed at Music City and distributed to all the local disk jockeys and have it reviewed on Al Jarvis' program the day Father Coughlin is a guest.[65]

Hey Toscanini was pretty hot. I guess you'd have just about died at *Tristan und Isolde*. I can't explain how good it was. The tempo, feeling, and everything, just seemed as right as it could be. It was a fine experience, [although] I would like to have had it with you. I happen to have had a date that night with Annie O'Grady and a friend. So your maledictions against my mythical companion are quite uncalled for—but nevertheless appreciated.

Your Mulberry bush routine is slightly confusing—as I presume you meant it to be. My only comment is that it's doubly confusing to be chasing around a mulberry bush and to meet someone going round the other way. With that little gem that I'm not sure I understand myself, I'll leave you with my undying love and a resolve to write a much more entertaining letter next time. Please write soon. You are a swell letter writer you are.

Love,
Stotesbury

April 30, 1945
Stotesbury Darling,

I have just finished two shows in this B.O. palace and have three more to go.[66] Gad, the days just go on and on, and I keep singing "I Should Care"—and I do, I *really* do. Do you want to know what time the first show goes on in this torture chamber? Well sir, at 10:45 [a.m.]. You know from various phone conversations that I cannot even talk at that time of day let alone sing. Honestly I sound like a frog having labor pains.

It was certainly nice of you all to phone the other evening. Except I got real lonesome after I hung up and was quite surly to everyone the remaining part of the p.m. Did you have a ball on the Colonna date?[67] That should be a pretty funny record. You sounded sorta high on the phone. Hope you didn't disgrace yourself or anything. You know how you get Paul.

The New York weather is keeping up its beat-up reputation. At the moment it's pouring. I don't know why California rain is so much more wonderful than New York [rain]. The sun has made a few feeble appearances the last few days, but it laid a big bomb so it retired to where ever it hides back here.

The audiences are still quite happy about me. Saturday and Sunday they were wonderful—all kids of course. There are a lot of kids here every day. I guess they just play hooky from school—blessings on them.

How about "Candy" being number one on the *Hit Parade* Saturday?[68] Guess we sure nailed that one. I'll bet your song is in the top three in the next couple of weeks—the kids love it. You oughta get pretty rich from it huh? John's piece is coming up fast too.[69] The way I watch the lists you'd think I wrote the songs. I even find myself smiling in a smug way. I can't see why I should care if your old songs are hits or not. It'll just make you guys more conceited than you already are; which makes both of you end up practically unbearable. I'm still happy about it though, I am.

Some girls cornered me the other day and wanted to know all about you. If I liked to work with you, what you looked like, and what sort of fellow you were. So I told them what a "peacheroo" you were. They seemed real pleased to find out you are such a swell fellow. I have a plan. I'm gonna start telling them that you and I are madly in love with each other. They'll undoubtedly tell all their friends and that way it'll get all over. I'll have you over a barrel then, won't I? There won't be much you can do about it unless you just want to be a plain cad. I'm gonna corner you sooner or later Weston. By hook or by crook, you might as well stop fighting me boy. I'm very determined. You're one of the few people who can talk me in and out of things, but you aren't here and letters just won't fill the bill. If you should hear that we're engaged or anything don't do a double take or scream. Just smile and say, "You'll have to ask Miss Stafford about that." Leave the rest to me. This, I think, is probably the cleverest, most darling idea my little head has thought of in a long time. Excuse me now as I have to go act and sing at the same time.

I went over to the hotel after the show and got your wire. Glad you liked my solo, but you do see what I'm up against with those other things.

The only thing that saved me from that closing saga was the Paramount schedule. I'm gonna show Mike your wire and tell him when they have the meeting concerning the show to try and get me out of at least that closing thing. They have one every week. He already thinks I shouldn't do it and your wire will help cinch it. I don't know if I can get out of the duet though. Wish I could, Larry Brooks is a real swell person, but we don't see eye-to-eye on musical matters.[70] He's a square, I thought so from the beginning. But yesterday I found out for sure. The band was playing some hot music, a la Robert Russell Bennett, and Larry started singing licks. The licks were bad enough, but he was saying "zazz zoo zazz" at the same time. How much can a body stand when they're away from home. They are very nice to me however. Nevertheless, I wish something would come up and save me from that show every Sunday. All I can think is how swell Cadillac cars are. I never did like Fords.

Next Sunday I'm on the Borden show too.[71] Should be a real exciting day. Two radio shows and five here at the Paramount. I'm doing the Martinique arrangement of "I Promise You." They wanted something that moved along and that sort of fit the bill—as they say in radio.[72]

Baby Doll, I made a trip over to Fifth Avenue the other day just to send you some cherry "chawclots" but the girl said they were very bad for shipping. If you want to take a chance I'll send some anyway. I couldn't figure which was worse. You sitting out there without them or receiving them all ruined. I can just see the look of horrified disbelief on your face if they were no good. You know how you bank on those things. If you want to take a chance though, I'm game. Leave me know your decision.

I thought you'd like to know that Norman Foley just phoned me.[73]

I just talked to the office and they said they hadn't heard from Jim [Conkling]. Maybe he's gone to Chicago or something. Hope not, he's such a nice boy. It'll certainly be good to see him.

Jeepers, what if I have to stay back here for a long time. I just get panicky when I think of it. Mike keeps saying do it now and get it over. But he doesn't know that I have a crush on you. If I'm here a long time won't you have to come back and make records with me? Because I just won't make them without you and that's that. If you did come back it's such a long trip that it only stands to reason you'd stay a while—say six months or so. I wish I wouldn't have to stay. I miss my little car, my little house, the office and the Prez, and your poor little eyes and chest and you too.

Eh law, there isn't anything else to write that I can think of. Write me soon or I shall perish. I know this typing of mine is a scandal to the hooty owls; but I write such long letters when I write you and my poor little shoulder gets too tired with a pen.

Love,
Fatso

P.S. The Toscanini concert sounds wonderful. I would have loved *Tristan*. I'm not too familiar with it except parts, but the parts I know I think are wonderful. Maybe we can hear it sometime, huh?

[May 3, 1945]⁷⁴
Elspeth dearest,⁷⁵

Your lengthy and extremely clever little epistle received and contents noted. First I must elaborate on my wire a bit. The first tune was really swell and I can stomach the duets as long as he doesn't have you doing that "delayed arrangement" type of singing (following the band with the melody) that went out with Stanley Steamers.⁷⁶ There's just no excuse for you getting mixed up in those last extravaganzas that close the program.

N.Y.C. Paramount Theatre marquee for *Salty O'Rourke* (ca. May 1945).

I really think that could hurt you, even though most of your type of fans are chasing each other through the woods on Sunday afternoon. Some of them might be home sick and tune in. Or it might rain. And if they ever heard you singing "Three Blind Mice" you'd be as dead as Dick Todd.[77]

Nothing much new here. Margaret Whiting was in to see about making records.[78] How many girl vocalists can we have?! [She] asked about "Wait and See" and I told her we were holding it for you—waiting for your voice to change.[79]

Just got some more ink.[80] I guess I'd just die if you could send some more cherries. I don't care if they be squashed or leaky—I'll eat 'em anyway. Have been seeing quite a bit of Ax and we are threatening to come up with a follow-up to "I Should Care."[81] "Dream" is to be on the *Hit Parade* this week and I am very thankful for that. If "I Should Care" had made it first I'd be Musicraft's new office boy.[82]

We struggled lamely through an unfunny [Jerry] Colonna date. The two martinis and our call to you were our high spots of the day—and not in that order either.

Palm Springs was pretty hot. John is there now and will be there for a week. He and Glenn [Wallichs] both liked the *Ford Show* very much. They are much more resigned to you becoming the poor man's Vivian Della Chiesa than I am. Maybe I take a more personal interest—who knows? I'd hate to see you get tied up there and as a result of that miss out on your own show. But Mike knows what he's doing in that department. And no matter what happens I still think you're real nice. And why don't you come back to California and stop trying to be so successful? The above is a completely ridiculous statement. Mike is right, now is the time to do it.

I'm on Al Jarvis' review program on Saturday and will probably throttle Dexter before it's over.[83] Will write more later. Am mad about you and also love Chris is that ok?

So long,
Paul

May 11, 1945
Dearest Heart O'Mine,

I think that is an apropos salutation for you because it's sort of Irish and so are you. I must however admit the German sticks out more than the other. I figure though that if I keep harping on the Irish then someday that may predominate and all hell may break loose. As [the Irish] are known to be a very sentimental race of people. And that's how darkies were born, to say nothing of the birth of the blues.[84]

As for me, I'm half English and half dead. I've had two of my spells this week. I didn't fall down this time—I just almost did. These were followed by the most God-awful shakes, like the ones I had on the program that memorable day when I was glad there was you.[85] Natch, they happened on the stage. Couldn't take place in some nice quiet closet—oh no. I'm a regular damned side show [attraction], with the whole Paramount audience getting the benefit of my goings on. The first time I was so bad that I had to tell the people I wasn't feeling very well, but I would try to sing for them. Luckily it was a house full of kids and that me quite a heroine. So they proceeded to tear the house down with applause. The second time I was able to stop the shakes before it was noticeable to the public. It acts like a bad case of nerves to me. That is very puzzling though. I've certainly been anything but a nervous person all my life. So why all of a sudden should I start in on such as this. Anyway, come Monday morning I'm off to the doctors. I wouldn't fool with it except for all the weight I've lost in the past year and am still losing with no reason. I'll leave you know if you are going to see me again in my next letter. Wouldn't it be awful if I became one of those boring women who go around talking about their "spells." I see I have referred to them as such above. I must get a hold of myself.

Tomorrow heralds the arrival of my illustrious niece Tootsie, and my idiot sister Bette. Do you know we haven't received a wire or anything from those two dopes? If the L.A. office of G.A.C. hadn't wired us we'd be completely in the dark.[86] I suppose they think they can just waltz in to any old hotel in town and ask for a room. What are they crazy or something? We oughta just let 'em wander around Grand Central for a couple of hours tomorrow morning. That'd put the fear of God in them. It's no wonder outsiders sometimes refer to us as a family who do things in a strange and mysterious manner. It's an unwritten law in our group never to tell anyone anything—let alone each other. They will undoubtedly have a perfectly dreamy stay—to put it in their vernacular. In N.Y. neither of them have ever been anywhere before. "Bee" went to San Francisco on the train once and "Toots" has never been on one in her life. So you can imagine what a hysterical trip they're probably having. The porters and stewards will think the world is coming to an end—what with the scarcity of tips, etc. All I ask is that they get the right train out of Chicago. I'm not too worried with Tootsie on the scene. She'll ask folks about things she doesn't understand. "Bee" is just like I used to be. She'd let them put her on any old train going any old place rather than ask anyone.

You should have the records by now. I'm anxious to know what you think of them. You'll probably think they just smell. I also sent you some cherry "chawclots." I hope they arrive with something left in them. The store was very distressed at sending them at all.

Just talked to Miss Kurts up at the office. She said Jim [Conkling] had arrived and was over in Jersey now. He'll be in N.Y. on Monday.

By the way, George Simon wants to know what you think of that small combo that's on the back of one of those records of mine. It's some group he found here in N.Y. He sure wants to go to work for Capitol. He really thinks it's a wonderful company. I just sit around and look smug because I already work for them.

Baby doll, I certainly did gobble up those dates you sent us. They were so good. The plain were pretty hot, but those fancy jobs are just out of this world. Did you get some for yourself? Because you'd like them. Besides being so good I felt real healthy when I ate them. And if I was home I'd go right down to the back room at Capitol and give Chas. Wick a real hot kiss for being so thoughtful. It has been quite a while since I've had a kiss from the gentleman. As I remember, they ain't no flies on 'em. That ought to make you pretty conceited for the next hour or so.

I forgot to wire you that the arr. arrived okay. But you'll know by the time this letter gets there that it did—more exciting that way.

I have to get dressed now. Write me real soon or I'll get morose. Might even get a case of the "screaming dirties." I still have an awful acute crush on you and hope you are the same. By the way I'm buying all the furniture at Pauline's place—including that piano. Guess that should put me up a notch or two in your book. You like the piano pretty much anyway.

Love,
Wadhead

[May 13, 1945][87]

Dear Josie-Anne Sweetheart,

Well first of all guess what arrived and is wonderful—the box of cherry chocolates. Hardly a morsel of juice leaked out; and they taste so fine—the best I ever seen anywhere. Boy you were sure swell to send them; and I do appreciate it I do. Then secondly, you were wonderful today on the *Ford Show*. I hate to keep telling you this if you don't like it, but baby you sing the hell out of that kind of music; and it will be going on long after Al Donahue has shot Dave Dexter and we are once again at peace.[88] I went on Jarvis' show and Dex and I had some keen words—as I guess I told you before. However he is a fine lad; and if we round off his edges a little he may make it.

On the overseas news department, Bing called yesterday and wanted to know if I wanted to go overseas with Dixie[89]—who is planning to take a troupe out. It is supposed to last eight weeks; and I told him that sometime along thru there I was supposed to go to New York and make some records with you. He wanted to know all about you and the theaters; how you were doing there, etc. Said he knew you'd do well there—seems to be quite a fan. I don't think he's going to go at all now because he has to start the Irving Berlin picture soon.[90]

Our little idea, which you and Glenn and I talked about so furiously in New York, has been broached to Buddy [De Sylva] and John and has received very enthusiastic reception. Glenn is waiting until Buddy finishes his picture to go into it further. Of course by then you'll be much too big to even speak to us; but we may consult you technically from time to time.

I have a small secret to confide in you alone, which is mute testimony to my undying devotion. One of Dinah's trusted lieutenants contacted me last week about taking over the show in the fall and also handling the records for her. I declined the latter with no regrets and know that I won't get far with the former because I will have to insist on a deal whereby none of the arrangements I make for her can be used on records. This will make me as popular as Himmler; and so I don't imagine anything will happen. But as soon as you have any hopes of any action let me know at once; because I don't want to get mixed up with her or Cass Daley and then have to miss out on something we'd like to do together. I use the word "together" because no matter what happens between you and Mike we'll still be friends and there's no reason in the world why we can't work together in perfect harmony.

Now don't fly off the handles at this—but if we had to, would you make a side or two while Jim [Conkling] is in New York in case we just need one for your next release? I haven't talked to the Prez because he's been in Palm Springs for a couple of weeks, but if your record comes out in a couple of weeks in New York we may need another release along about August or September; and that means getting the records made sooner than Glenn and I had planned to come to New York. I will talk it over with the Prez and then consult you. So don't get excited until you hear further from me. The main thing, as always, is that you be kept extremely happy. After all, I didn't listen to you scream at "Moss" and "Bullets" all those times and not learn something from it.⁹¹

The Prez has been playing for about two weeks [in Palm Springs]—as I mentioned above. I've talked with him on the phone several times, and he seems alternately gay as hell and extremely mad at the world. The latter mood was mostly caused by Stan Kenton, who after Mercer and I picked out several tunes for him, wound up making "Tampico" and an instrumental.⁹² The temperamental artistes. [For example,] whatever happened to Ella Mae? She went on the Jarvis show and said all she'd like to have for an accompaniment would be a rhythm section. And next date Jack, she's going to get just that: Tex Ritter on guitar, Candy Candido on bass, Little Jack Little on piano, and Phil Harris on drums.⁹³ What a dame? Glenn's wife saw her in Saks the other day in tight shorts; and in tight shorts she is no bargain.⁹⁴

I'm having a little gathering of the clan for Mickey [Goldsen] this evening as sort of a sendoff for his trip back East.⁹⁵ He was with John for a while at Palm Springs and had a wonderful time. John really lived last night with "Dream" and "Laura" number two and three.⁹⁶ I got quite a kick out of "I Should Care" making it—phony as it may be. As my Father said, "Jo's doing that song five times a day at the Paramount hasn't hurt it any." Much as I hate to I must admit my indebtedness.

Walter Hannan, the bard of Beverly Hills, has written a beautiful lyric to that tune I've had for some time—the sort of minor [key] one. And I'm waiting to show it to the Prez. Hope he likes it because I really do. I'll send it to you if you'd like to see it. Naturally Martha [Tilton] got the first copy last week; and I'd better immediately admit I'm kidding.

Are you definitely set on the *Ford Show*? And if so, for how long? R.S.V.P. You really sound better than I've ever heard you before. I got quite knocked out today and that is a rare experience for me in my old age. Naturally I pine for you continually—probably in vain. But time will tell as the poets never say. Tell Chris her letter was a killer and I shall answer soon. And keep singing like that baby—you're wonderful. Write soon—and at length. And thanks again for the chocolates. I'm going right out and eat one right now—the approved way of course. Let the candy down into your mouth by the stem and then let it slowly dissolve. So long, I've got to hurry...

Love,
Childredge

[May 14, 1945][97]
Hey baby,

What is going on with you? I was just about to mail my letter when yours arrived. I am much disturbed by all the fainting, shaking, etc. No kidding, that's really bad. What are you doing about it? If whatever doctor you go to doesn't give you a basal metabolism test at once I shall scalp not only him, but you and Chris too. Maybe even Pauline, Tootsie, and crazy Bette Jane the mad woman.

I was pretty unhappy to hear about it. In my book you ain't a fainting gal and something should be done about it immediately. I don't guess it's much to worry about. Probably by the time you've received this you've been to a doctor and discovered all you need is some extra goat's milk and a few cocaine capsules. But can I help it if I get excited? Maybe you just better cancel out all [work] and come home. Or don't you like starving to death? I personally blame Robert Russell Bennett, Esq. for the whole thing. But who am I to judge? Please advise me at once as soon as you hear what goes.

Miss you and will let you know as soon as the trip East either takes visible form or fades into nothingness.

Love,
Rudolpho[98]

May 23, 1945
Dearest Westinghouse love bug darling,

Here I sit with three pages of a letter all typed out and now I have to start from scratch on account of last night's phone conversation. Do you know we talked for forty-five minutes? The operator called me back and informed me of the fact. I felt like asking her if she thought that would make me sleep better or something. As for my sleeping last night, I didn't do very well. I think I finally dropped off about eight this morning. I've come to the conclusion that I should never come close to arguing with you. It upsets me too much. I know that when I'm through I'll still love you. But you're such a funny bug you're liable to say, "she's an old dumb girl and I won't like her anymore." Did you Paul? Huh Paul, did you?

It was wonderful talking to the Prez and you the other day. Every time I hear that "down souf" talk of his I get so homesick I could just fold up and die. I've decided that life is too short and folks shouldn't have to be away from home when they don't want to be. And a lot of good that decision will do me. Mike is absolutely no comfort on the subject. When I start singing the blues about being away from home he just gives me the long steady look until I sorta dwindle off. Oh well. Kismet, where is he playing this week?[99]

Isn't it dumb for me to have anemia? One thing that I like about the whole thing is the doctor says I can't diet until I get my blood and blood pressure back to normal. That'll take about two months. And is Mike ever burned up. He wants me to take off about twenty-five more pounds and be a big movie queen. I can't convince him that I couldn't possibly take off that much weight. Talk about your hank of hair. I haven't weighed that little since I was 3'11" tall and about six-years-old. You know Paul how my poor little bones stick out now? Can you imagine how they'd be if I lost that much more weight? Anyway, for the time being I've got the old boy over a barrel. He still looks very unhappy when I order "chawclot" sundaes though. So I don't have them very often.

I wish you'd hurry up and come back here. I wish you'd leave right now—while you're reading this sentence. I wish I was a femme fatal and guys just couldn't resist me and would take airplanes and too many sleeping tablets on my account. But they don't, they just say, "Well I'm getting cold feet now. Maybe I shouldn't come back there at all. I don't want to get mixed up in your problems." And stuff like that. Of course, this whole thing with Mike is probably all my fault. I should have straightened the situation out right at first. Like I told you I was going to, but it is easy to get into those things—at least it is for me. I'm such a soft for people I'm fond of and I'm certainly fond of Mike. I kept telling myself I had to do something. And wondering at the same time how I was gonna do it without hurting his feelings. I've gone out with him a lot simply because I don't know anyone else and no one else asks me out. He asked me to marry him not too long ago. I said no of course. I don't know how to make my sentiments much clearer to him than that. I suppose I could stop seeing him socially, but I work pretty hard and it's nice to go out and relax and have a few laughs. I don't know much about Mike's past romantic life, but surely the man has taken girls out before. So why should everyone take the attitude that something is "gonna happen between you two."

As far as being serious on my part, it's just ridiculous. In the first place my family would have a mass epileptic fit. Meanwhile everywhere we go all his friends smile at us knowingly and say "my what a peachy pair." And I wish I was dead. I feel like I'm being backed into a corner and I don't know how to get out of it. At this point, my main concern is Mike's feelings. Honestly Paul, he's about the most terrific guy I've ever known. He's just wonderful and I'd almost rather die than really hurt him. I may be making a fool of myself to think he cares that much. But I don't think so. Staying back here so long isn't gonna help matters any either. Anyway, I'm plenty panicky and I don't know what to do. I wish I was home I do. I'm scared I am.

Paul, why do I always get into jams? Other people seem to live fairly normal lives, but ever since I came back here awful things have been happening to me. Except when you were here baby doll. So if you ask me you'd better either tell me to get lost or get back here and straighten me out—one or the other. Or are you just bored with the whole situation? If you are I don't blame you. Shirl-girl is a nice girl and I wish she'd never left Toledo.[100]

I wish you could have heard the arrangement of "Beginning to See the Light." Sunday—it was pretty funny—I could hardly sing. They thought it was just wonderful though. The producer and Bennett kept smiling at each other and talking about how they were really gonna surprise a few people coming on the air with that [arrangement]. I'll bet they surprised a few people all right. In fact family doctors are probably still trying to revive music lovers throughout the states. That arranger ought to be shot. He just sat there beaming though and patting his damned feet—one, three, one, three, one, three. I expected him to pull out a reefer any minute and light up—eh law.

The weather is beautiful today and it's about time. It has done nothing but rain for four weeks. It's a little on the muggy side, but not enough to be uncomfortable.

I changed my hairline. You know how my hair grew down too low on my forehead? Well sir I didn't do a thing but get burned one night and shave it off. I'm gonna have to have it done some way so it'll be permanent. But I just wanted to see how I'd look with it changed. Everyone says it's a big improvement. I now have a nice broad intelligent forehead, which will fool everyone but you. No one else knows that I don't know what fifteen and seven are off hand; and don't you tell them either. It makes my face look longer and takes away some of that beach ball baby-face look. I'm sophisticated I am.

I haven't been able to reach Mike this morning on the Randy Brooks thing.[101] He'll probably call before long though and I'll do my best. Really though darling, you're wrong about Mike and the Decca deal. Wherever he puts Randy it'll be because he thinks it's the best place for Randy. He can be young of course, [and] no one can be right all the time. He's looking at it from a cold business standpoint. You and I feel differently about the company. I think it's the only one and so do you. I feel sorry for everyone who works for anyone else. But Mike had to be sold and convinced that it's the best deal for Randy. And evidently so far Decca has done the best job on that score.

Say by the way, there is talk around Toots Shor's that Capitol is gonna sell out to Jules Stein.[102] Have you heard anything about that? I heard the other day that Stein had everyone convinced but John—including De Sylva.[103] I may shoot myself if that's true. I just laughed heartily at the man and said, "Are they kidding?" And then privately heaved my lunch. Let the world come to an end, let the heavens fall in, but don't let's sell our pride and joy. Jeepers.

Did you get the clipping Mike sent to you? He thought it was very funny and keeps asking me if you got it.

Well, long distance love life, I've gotta get dressed and go sing through my nose. Please, with sugar, write me real fast. I guess I'd just die of joy if you came back with Glenn on the 3rd. And even if I am only a black protestant my prayers are going like mad. Maybe where you're concerned I ought to do my praying over in St. Patty's.[104] Write soon sweetheart. And remember, you're for me.

Love,
Jo-Ann

P.W. and Shirley Mitchell attend Stan Kenton's opening at the Hollywood Palladium (November 1944).

[May 28, 1945][105]
Dearest Jo-Ann Honey Sweetheart,

    After hearing the *Ford Show* today I imagine Chris is more unbearable and insufferably conceited than ever before. What with having anyone so famous and charming as Larry Brooks pronounce her name from coast to coast. My surprise was only exceeded when you started talking and sounded as if you had the original *code in by head*.[106] Your singing sounded wonderful. How in hell you can sing like that with such a cold I'll never understand. That Paramount is an awful job. You'd better get plenty of sleep, stay out of cabarets, drink double-rich malted milks, and smoke plenty of weed—or else you'll never lose that cold. And what's more it will get worse. And what am I doing sounding like Dr. Christian except that I don't want you to get sick? And gee you're anemic already.

    As for our phone conversation, I never really was under the impression we even had an argument. I would say rather a "nice spirited chat," which I thoroughly enjoyed. Your loyalty is charming at all times, whether directed at Capitol, Mike, or Oscar Leiss. And I love you for it. At the time of writing this I don't know whether we have Randy Brooks or not. But no matter what happens you are still the number one character in the Capitol family.

    Things are happening thick and fast on that show; and I'll give you a Winchell-type summary. Flash! Sam Steiffel tells Wm. Morris that Pipers are NOT available for radio (so they can do that stale tour with Andy [Russell]). Lowery blows his top, and they ask for their release from both Wm. Morris and Sam S. who is rapidly becoming so brilliant that he is now known as the Jewish Ken Dolan.[107] (all this information is highly confidential)... Mercer meets (oh I forgot) Flash! Mercer meets with Norm Blackburn and Carroll Carroll and tells them he wants you and no nonsense;[108] but frankly neither of us really know what the hell is going on... (The Martha Tilton story is almost as absurd as my secret conviction that Mike planted the story so that you'd hate us and sign that deal with Musicraft Records that he's always talking about. I really think they're automatically ruling you out because of Ford and because of the fact that you are in the East.) Flash! We are supposed to make a wax within two weeks, but John and I are not too terribly enthusiastic because it looks as if it might get out of hand and we might wind up with some people we don't give a damn about. (The only trouble is that it knocks out our chance to leave for N.Y. real soon; as we can't make a move until we hear about making the wax.) So much for that junk.

I'm going to send you a copy of the Capitol [News] because Dex blew his top and wrote all about you and put your picture on the cover. And I feel pretty damn happy because all my beefing at least brought some action. Glenn is supposedly leaving on Sunday. And if a miracle happens and we get that show I'll have to come back there and record before we start. *If* we start in August. So keep your poor little bony anemic fingers crossed and I'll do the same. I told John about your call and we talked it all over and there really isn't very much we can do about it. If we tell Shaky he'll get all excited and do something very stupid like booking Herman on *Truth or Consequences*. So about all we do is appreciate the fact that you called and told us about it. John was disturbed about the Martha Tilton routine because that's just somebody's imagination. And as for the Jules Stein deal, that is the funniest laugh I've had since Charlie Wick played "Ac-Cen-Tchu-Ate" for the Pipers. Whenever you hear those rumors *don't believe nothing* 'til you check with us. And if there's anything momentous afoot you'll hear first baby. Even before Ella Mae or Harry Owens.

I thought Mike's clipping was really a killer. You should save one for your scrapbook—looks pretty damned impressive. I really think you're doing yourself a lot of good on Ford. You sound wonderful; and I've even got now so that I almost like Larry Brooks. The dialogue disturbs John somewhat. He doesn't think they make you sound natural enough. I also think that as far as your jitterbug audience is concerned we'll cover the field pretty thoroughly by having "Conversation" and "Sunny Side" come out one right after another. In other words you've very little to worry about. I sure can appreciate your problems, but am sure all will turn out OK. And it's better to talk about on the phone than for me to write about.

I guess that's about all except that we had a date with the Pipers and all the players—sort of old home week. [It was] a lot of fun. I guess our original set-up was too good to be true and we were lucky to have had six months of it. Sometimes I wish we'd settled down on South Vermont [Street] or wherever those beautiful houses were, then there'd be nothing to do but for me to work in the gas station. And you in the office of the telephone company or in the grocery store. And get real drunk Saturday nights and read comic magazines together and work in the garden on Sundays. How long do you think we could have stood it? Now you're going to spoil it all and go in the movies and undoubtedly marry Steve Crane and have your vocal chords inscribed in cement at Graumann's. If you haven't seen *The Clock*—and if it's still playing anywhere when you finish the Paramount—I think you'll like it.

Write me again soon. You still write wonderful letters. And I'll let you know just as soon as I know anything about New York. And I owe you a phone call too. For Pete's sake take care of yourself and get rid of that cold. Hope I get to see you real soon.

Love,
Renaldo[109]

[June 9, 1945][110]
Dear Honey-Baby Sweetie Pie,

Well, for twenty-four rather exciting hours yesterday I was all set to leave for New York two weeks from today, if not sooner, and then this morning Glenn called and said that the Prez had decided there wasn't enough to make a trip worthwhile—so it's all off. Naturally all this is highly confidential. Don't mention to the Prez any of the following routine, because you know him as well as I and he wants—and rightfully so—to figure the thing out his way. The way it looks now we won't make "Wait and See" at all. The only thing that disturbs Jim and me is that we don't know when you'll be getting another record—unless John picks some tunes for you in New York. Of course this can all change in one hour's notice and right now you probably know a lot more about it than I. It was pretty hot for a while yesterday to think that I'd be on my way so soon, but I still may make it sometime this summer; and I'll just unpack and settle down again.

I almost wired you last night to tell you I was coming. Lucky I didn't or I'd have had to wire you again today. Glenn seemed to want me to get back there, but I guess it is silly just for a couple of records. Or is it?! By the way, Jim suggests that Mike talk to John or Glenn or both—if the opportunity presents itself. Along the lines that he talked to Jim, concerning the fact that it is important for you to have another record before too long a time elapses. Naturally Mike isn't to quote Jim or me, but we both agree that now is the time for you to make your most determined effort. That Billboard poll was a killer; and I'm awful proud of you. I guess Mike knows what he's talking about when he says if you'll work you can "break it up." Also, Herman (Shaky's assistant) told me to tell you that they are working on some kind of a new deal for all of us and for Mike not to be surprised when they approach him. This new big deal will probably get no further than the back booth at the Tropics, but at least I told you.

This can't be a very long letter as I have to hurry to mail it. But I am quite disturbed over your reaction to *The Enchanted Cottage*, seeing as how it knocked me clean out. You've got to stop going to those kind of pictures with Mike and Tom Rockwell if that's the way they're going to affect you. Somewhere between eating peanuts and the newsreel you got the thing twisted. It said that if you're happily in love you are automatically beautiful and charming; unless the New York version of the picture is different from the Los Angeles one. I really don't think you're to be held responsible—only your environment. I bet that if you saw it in the Pantages you'd like it fine. If you're getting bitter back there you'll have plenty of explaining to do if and when (or when and if) I ever get there. And I haven't seen *Laura* yet so there. Jo, how do you like that for apples? You were real sweet to bother with that girl who wants to sing; and Mother has already heard from Pittsfield about it. So nice deeds come home at eventide. This is all for now. Once again don't mention the above to a soul. And let me know the set-up as soon as you hear anything. If necessary I'll mail the arrangement back there, but I won't have to like it. Will I Jo, hey? I'll write again cause this is short. Still hope to see you before October.

Love,
Harford

June 14, 1945
Dearest Baby Doll,

I started to write this letter about three hours ago and then Chris, the kids, and me started talking it up about the problems of life in general so now it's a fast four thirty in the a.m.

I'm glad I called you today. I felt better after I'd talked to you. I spent a horrible day yesterday. I just wandered all day trying not to be brought down. I actually had quite a weeping spell. Don't tell anyone that—it's confidential. I was gonna call yesterday but I knew darn well I'd cry over the phone if I did—now you know. Weston, I have to be pretty upset to get in that state. I'm finding out in my old age that I don't take to changes very well. All I could think of yesterday was I wanna go home, I don't want to make lots of money, I don't want to be famous, I hate New York, I'm mad at the Prez, and I love Paul dearly. Well I tho't and tho't and decided that the world wouldn't come to an end. At least I don't *think* it will. I'm still not thoroughly convinced. Don't be mad at the Prez though honey. You should know him by now. As I said today, you and I decided a long time ago that you just have to accept him as he is or not at all. Just remember what a wonderful guy he is. He just has some idea in his pixie mind and when he's like this there isn't any use in trying to change him.

I've seen him like this with other people. I've never run into it myself before, but as I told you his whole attitude is very strange —very business-like and detached, etc. I can't ever forget, however, what he's done for me and what I owe him. So in this case as much as I hate it—and believe me darling I hate it—I'll have to do what he wants. Please don't be too mad at John. Try to understand. So much for that.

I've been seeing a lot of shows since I got out of the Paramount. I've seen *Dear Ruth*, which was wonderful; *Up in Central Park* (are they kidding?); *Song of Norway*—Larry Brooks has the lead in that (he was very good and I enjoyed it); I saw *The Glass Menagerie* tonight—it's a strange play, but Laurette Taylor was just wonderful; *Dark of the Moon*, which is a hillbilly legend and full of hillbilly folk music—and natch I was right at home. I'm seeing *Carousel* Friday and will leave you know.[111]

I was sort of pleasantly surprised with the Billboard poll.[112] Mike sent [Tom] Rockwell a copy through the mail and asked him what more he wanted. He's really raising holy hell up at that office and told Rockwell the other day in so many words that he wasn't waiting much longer for something to happen for the fall. He was sure if they couldn't do anything some other office could. He can sure raise a stink when he gets mad.

I'm on Texaco this coming Sunday. I'm doing "Laura" and some other tune we haven't decided on yet. As the producer said today, "something light and spirited, but not too low down." How are you, the Lord knows what I'll end up with. Maybe "Mexicali Rose" in fox trot time, "God Bless America," and maybe I'll do away with myself tonight.

We discussed that Jill Warren episode today in a very kidding manner.[113] However, to be serious for a moment, I trust I don't have to tell you I'd never say anything that would cause you any trouble. Firstly, because I'm much too fond of you. Secondly, leave us face it, I don't know anything to say—coda.

Shades of Pearl Harbor, they're selling the place where we live out there. The new land lords may be very willing to have us stay on and then again they may not—which usually happens. Needles to say, at present the entire Stafford clan, eastern branch, wishes they were dead. Seven rooms of furniture is no laughing matter when you have no place to put it but the middle of Orange Drive. I worry about those things Paul. My main concern is the piano, which I told you I was gonna buy. If you didn't have your grand I'd just let you have it and you could play pieces on it 'til I come home. This Pollyanna sentence is followed by a hoarse *Pagliacci* sort of laugh.[114] The only room at your place would be the badminton court and I'll be damned if I'll allow that. Anyway, utter confusion reigns. However that state of mind—I'm still talking of utter confusion—has become such a familiar emotion to me in the past six months that I'll probably be able to cope with this new problem very intelligently. My name is "Carrie Flint [and] I've come to tea."[115] Has anyone got some marijuana that's already lit?

Listen, man-of-my-denied dreams, it is broad daylight and I'm real sleepy. So write me quick. I know there should be an "ly" on that word, that 15 + 7 is 22—and I have a big crush on you.

Love,
Jo Ann

June 19, 1945
Dearest Punkin' Face,

I just wish you could get a load of this weather. It is raining so hard outside that I'm sure it'd knock a person down if they walked in it. While this is going on I have every window in the place up and all the fans going and I still can't breathe. Make some sense out of that if you can. I'm listening to a murder mystery on the radio and I'm pretty scared. But the sound of the typewriter sort of cheers me up. All the family have gone to see *The Voice of the Turtle*.[116]

I don't owe you a letter so therefore I shouldn't be writing. But as you've often told me, you are such a charming person. So I guess that's why I'm writing.

Well sir, tomorrow is my record date. I'm really not very excited about it. Sy couldn't do any of the arrangements.[117] Eddie Sauter is doing one, Bob Haggart another, and another fellow that I don't know is doing the others.[118] We tried to pick as commercial type tunes as we could find. I really like one of them, "Gee, It's Good to Hold You"—Capitol publishes it. I guess I told you about it on the phone.

The Prez finally came around the other day and was his old, sweet self. I asked him what he had been building and he informed me that I should know him and his moods by now. So one just shrugs one's shoulders and controls one's desire to hit him in the head. When we were looking over tunes we came across one from the forthcoming picture *State Fair*, called "That's for Me" (it's by Hammerstein and Rodgers). And Paul I think it's one of the prettiest songs I've ever heard. John said, "Well, if you like it so much, why don't you record it?" I told him I'd love to but there was only one person in the world I'd record that song with. And unless he wanted a weeping woman on his should not to suggest anything else. He asked me if I meant you and I told him I didn't mean Robert Russell Bennett. So he calmly says, "Well, I'm pretty sure he'll be back here sometime next month. You can do it then and back it up with 'Wait and See,'—that is if you want to." Natch, I mentally awarded him the medal for the man most likely to succeed in 1946.

Have they said anything about you coming back next month yet? If you can get a copy of the tune, get one and play it. I think the lyric is simply wonderful too. The opening line says, "I saw you standing there, and you were something to me." Ain't that a killer? I hope you like it. It'd be terrible if you didn't—after me building it up so. Wouldn't it? Huh Paul, huh?

I saw *Carousel* the other night. It's a pretty good show—good music. And I've always loved the story of *Liliom* anyways. Anyways is the same sort of word as "anywheres" and is always used by those in the know—or in the Stork Club. Or "How are you Mr. Wilson?," which is a line from *Harvey* that I love also.

I'm now listening to *Fibber McGee and Molly*. And so help me if they get much more "folksy." I'm gonna ruin the rug.

I'm going to Atlantic City tomorrow after the record date and swim in the ocean I am. I'm gonna stay a couple of days. It'll do me good. Everything will be fine if I can get up the nerve enough to put on my new bathing suit. I've been buying bathing suits for six years now and then not getting up enough nerve to put them on. In spite of the weight I've lost I'm still not what one would call a "sweater girl." I'll let you know if I wore it or not. It's really quite a handicap because I love to swim. Eh law, the more I look at [it as a] handicap the more I'm convinced that should be a handicap—or is it either?

Did you hear me on the *Texaco Show* last Sunday?[119] I did "Laura" and "Yah Ta Ta." Bobby Warren made the arrangements and he did good too. Can you imagine Paul, I got a thousand dollars for the show. Isn't that ridiculous? I didn't give any of it back to them though.

I saw General Eisenhower today. They really gave him a welcome here. He rode Broadway in an open car and he stood up and waved to everyone.

This is the chummiest hotel in this hot weather. We live on the court, everyone keeps their windows wide open, and there are three soldiers who think I'm "cuter than a bugs ear" right across the way. I refuse to pull the blinds and smother just on account of them. I'm gonna get mad pretty quick and give them a piece of my mind. Or don't you think I can spare it. I'm gonna do something desperate though.

The kids left last week, got home Sunday, [and] talked to them yesterday. "Tootsie" said all Christopher would say to her for hours was that he didn't like her. I suppose he was rather insulted because she was gone so long. He probably isn't fit for shooting after spending that long a time with Mama who thinks all children are born to play with and have their own way. Whenever any form of discipline is suggested she informs us that she raised five that way and she has no complaints which naturally leaves you with nothing much to say.

Well, I can think of nothing else that would interest you except I miss you and would like very much to see you and hear you say, "Yeah Jo, yeah? Maybe I will before long." Huh Paul, huh?

Perspirationally yours,
Gladys

June 29, 1945
Dearest Baby Doll Creampuff, (yipes)

$65,000 home indeed. Sing to you at night—I'll say. If I hear of you having anything to do with that frustrated, over-hormoned, dirty talking girl, I may do away with myself. I can picture you now, Mr. and Mrs. Weston having a family get together at your Mother's on Sunday afternoon with new Mrs. Weston being—as you put it—her usual charming self. And give me a drag off of that before you put it out! In all fairness I'll have to admit the gal is stacked up pretty good and is a fair looking chick. But we mustn't let the sex angle overwhelm us. Or have we lost our heads completely?

You mentioned that I hadn't offered anything quite as exciting as the "blonde-*bum*shell." Well Sire, I'm the strong, silent type. I just sit back and let people slowly appreciate me. I grow on you Paul. But as long as there is sort of a contest on as to who would make you the charmingest wife in the whole wide world; I may as well list what I think are my most adorable traits. Being as I'm probably the laziest human on the face of the you know what. I'd never be caught cluttering up the house with dust rags, vacuum cleaners, etc. 'Course the house might be a little dirty, granted, but by the same token I wouldn't be all tuckered out from housework and you wouldn't be in danger of falling over brooms and breaking your poor little head. [Also], I can only cook chili and beans. You don't like them so there wouldn't be any dirty dishes on the sink because I wouldn't be doing any cooking whatsoever. We could be "social butterflies" and eat out *all* the time. Whenever I'd have to get up real early in the morning I'll promise you right now I'd sing very quietly. I always sing "Oh, What a Beautiful Morning," when I have to get up early. But as I said, I'd be very careful to sing softly and you'd hardly be able to hear me at all. Unless of course you were trying very hard. If you wanted to hear [me], all you'd have to do is say, "I can't hear you baby," and I'll sing louder. The only thing I can think of that we might argue about is two-beat and four-beat. One sure way of getting rid of that possibility would be to not have any of the aforementioned rhythms around the place. Just go in for strictly waltzes. They are nearly always in three-beat, so there would be no argument. Wayne King has a lot of nice albums and we could spend many afternoons eating Indian nuts and listening.

As far as the $65,000 home is concerned. Those places on south Figueroa are a lot more compact. Now you think of all these things over and because I'm a fair-minded person, I'll just say, may the best woman win. One more point in my favor, in a pinch I can do my own hair and nails.

I guess John decided he didn't like the records I made last week. He called this morning and said I had another record date next Monday.[120] Johnnie Johnston is having a session that day and I'll do a couple the same day.[121] From what I can gather the instrumentation will be like we had on "Long Ago." No brass, [except for] only on my sides we'll have one trumpet (Billy Butterfield). I'm remaking Mickey's tune, "Gee, It's Good to Hold You," and the tune I told you about from *State Fair*.[122] I told John I'd like to make it, but not unless I could make it with you. He evidently chose to ignore this impudent statement because he informed I was making it this morning. Sometimes I think John is afraid I'm gonna get too big for my britches or something. Because at the slightest indication of me "making a stand" about anything he really lets me have it—in his own inimitable, sarcastic way. Sort of "leave us not forget who's boss"—as if I ever would, however. Whatever he says or does I'm sure he's doing it because he thinks that's best for me. When I start to lose my patience with him I just stop and think; for the grace of God and Johnny Mercer I might still be doing one nighters and singing lead with a quartet. And I don't mean that to sound disrespectful to the Pipers either, but my present set-up is better naturally. Both John and Glenn seem to think you are just too busy out there to get back here any time in the near future. Whenever I bring up the subject they start reeling off the stuff you have to get out of ending up always with "and besides he *has* to have his tonsils out." Lots of things have come between us Paul, including 3,000 miles of U.S.A. and various blondes, but I'll be darned if in my wildest dreams I ever thought your tonsils would enter in to the picture. Are you coming back on your vacation? Huh Paul, huh?

My vacation to that garden spot of the East, Atlantic City, almost did me in. In my usual brilliant fashion I didn't use my head at all. You'd think anybody who hadn't been on a beach in several years would know to take it easy at first, but oh no, I was real eager beaver athlete. I frolicked on the sands two days in a row. It was over and under and then up for air for two or three hours each day. All was well until the night I came home. Then my forehead started swelling up, and I mean swelling. I thought the darned thing was gonna bust open. I looked like something out of Buck Rogers. Then the swelling left my head and moved down to my eyes. This was a real nifty effect—a Japanese spy sort of thing. After a few days of this routine I finally got the size of my face back to normal and then the peeling of many layers of scorched skin, Jack, started. For days I looked like a prehistoric decaying radish. At present I'm in fairly good shape except for a few million freckles. As for the great outdoors, the first one who says "get out and get under" may run into trouble. I shall stay inside and take vitamins.

I went to another doctor the other day for an examination. We found out that other one was wrong on some things so I decided I'd go someplace else. This one gave me one of those metabolism things you said I should have and a thorough general check up. He said I was perfect from stem to stern. Due to his cheering words I am now allowed to go on a diet. I can have all the radishes, carrots, and celery I can stow away. All the four-leaf clovers I can find in Central Park. He says I should lose five pounds the first week. I've got news for him. At this rate I'll fade away the first couple days. The only compensation for all this suffering being that the next time you see me I'll be so breath taking that Betty Hutton will be strictly with the bear. I only have to lose between ten and fifteen pounds though. So maybe I'll live through it. I've lost about seven pounds since you saw me. Which makes quite a bit of difference at this point. The doctor said I'd be more "peppy" too. Do you think I'd be more charming if I were more peppy?

Dad is having himself a ball. He's seen about everything that interests him, such as the Brooklyn Dodgers, the museum, Empire State, and R.C.A. He has tickets for *Harvey* tonight and *Oklahoma* on Monday, thanks to that miracle woman Mildred. I thought he'd like those two about as well as any of them. He ain't exactly the musical comedy type. He has two comments he makes on everything. The first being, "Well I'll be God Damned." This refers to the height of the buildings, etc. The other is less expressive, "hell-fire." Which when he says it comes out "hell-far." He'll be here until the eighth. We've certainly enjoyed having him. He's wanted to see New York all his life, but never really thought he'd get to. So it's like a fairy tale come true as far as he's concerned. And everything is so wonderful he can't believe it. It's wonderful to make something possible for a person like that. And one way of paying him back for doing so much for me all my life. I'm gonna bring Mama back as soon as we can talk her into coming. As far as she's concerned a trip to the grocery store practically involves packing a bag. But it would be good for her. And if one of us has to pretend we're dying to get her to come we will.

Love of my heart, I have to get dressed and go sell bonds in Jersey City now. Write me real soon. And if you have to get involved with girls, at least get involved with nice, clean ones.

I've been meaning in all my letters to remind you that you've never told me how much I owe you for the arranging you did for me on this last trip. Let me know because I can't stand unpaid bills. Another thing, I feel sort of funny about sending for the scores on songs like I've done a couple of times without paying you. After all they're the finest kind of arrangements. And when I do songs that you've arranged for me I like to have them. But there's no reason for me to have them for free. For instance, the *Ford Show* has "Alone Together" and "Yesterdays" programmed in the near future. They have arrangers natch, and they'll do them, but they won't be half as good as yours. So if we could make up a private deal on these things I'd feel much better about it. Leave me know, baby. "Out of This World" got here and thank you for sending it.

Say hello to your family and write me soon.

Love,
Slim

[July 9, 1945]
Dearest Jo-Ann Honey Sweetheart,

Have just listened to the *Ford Show* and Chloe just about did me in. I was barely able to recover in time for "Out of this World," but you really fractured that tune—sounded wonderful. And the other tunes on the show were great too. [I] see they have you doing four songs altogether. Pretty soon Larry Brooks can keep his overshoes, mackinaw, and toque on all weekend—in addition to every night in *Song of Norway*. I really think that show has been fine for you. I don't know why in hell I say that, because I don't know anything about the Hooper, or what type of people hear it. But I do know you sound terrific on it; and that should be enough. Gee I'm sounding like a fan. This is not at all in line with the traditional Weston policy of "tell 'em nothing, make believe everything stinks, and show no enthusiasm whatsoever." I must watch it.

We are expecting the arrival of the executive today on the Chief.[123] Glenn finally had to forsake the Southern Pacific; and for all I know "Atchison" is already paying off in railroad reservations. We hear all sorts of horrible rumors about how no-one can possibly get out of N.Y. for months and months. But the only thing that worries me is that if I take this show and you stay in N.Y. we may not get to make any records together, including the album, for twenty or thirty years. This is somewhat discouraging, but I'll see what Glenn has to say when I talk with him. Did the Prez say anything about your album when he was back there? Now is the time. And if we can make one with Andy [Russell] and Ella Mae and Tex [Ritter] and Harry Owens—why not you?

I'm still trying to get my tonsils out. I was all set this week after Margaret O'Brien, but now I have to do Jarvis' little radio gem on Saturday. I suppose I'll have to try and match wits with Dexter again. They now have a studio audience and everyone is trying harder for laughs than ever and paying little attention to the records. Dex told Abe Lyman to take the corn tassels out of his ears last week. So anything can happen this week.

In reply to your lengthy and at times sarcastic comments regarding my projected matrimonial venture with the incendiary—oh the hell with it—blonde. I have a few little additions to make. The way it looks now, I think I will wait until I see the type of job the decorator will do with her $65,000 home. After all it might not fit my personality. And besides it gives me an out in case I get a little wary. The thought of you emerging as a peppy type is something I never quite happened to think of before—and it slowed me down no end. Sporting in the surf, tennis, golf—who knows—in time even shuffle board and croquet. Why you'd wear a body out almost as quick as Hutton. And in what most folks consider much more unpleasant types of exercise. So you can see my mental turmoil is acute. In short, after all the con[versation] I'm getting about your new figure, face, and personality, I am getting exceedingly curious—I don't mind admitting. And I may have to come back there on an investigation trip to find out just what is going on. I can expect a report from Glenn, but it might be a little more objective than what I'm looking for. And somehow I wouldn't think to ask the Prez. And maybe my tonsils aren't so bad after all.

Axel and I have a box at the Bowl for Stokowski this summer, and tomorrow night is the first concert: *Tristan und Isolde* and the Tchaikovsky *Sixth*—which should be a good enough program for anyone except maybe Leonard Feather and Barry Ulanov.

Sammy Cahn is getting married! Big wedding at the Beverly Hills Hotel in September. So that leaves Axel without a roommate or an apartment. We've been sailing quite a bit and won our first race a month or so ago. But last week Ax and Ken Lane got tangled up with the spinnaker at a very inopportune moment and we lost the race—and nearly lost Ken overboard. I tried golf again last week for the first time in months, since I started slaving in the Capitol salt mines on a ten-hour-a-day basis.

Later...

Got a wire from Mike telling me I'd better take the show as long as it wasn't on an exclusive basis. So I guess I'll tell them today. I know I'll hate Joan Davis most of the time, but I guess I'll live thru it. I'll just be completely money-mad and think of nothing but loot. Speaking of loot, I don't know what to do about those arrangements. You're welcome to use them. So just let me know what you need. I'll send you a bill for the other ones I made for you when I write Chris, which will be soon. Because somewhere along the road of life she has developed the idea that we are ex-chums and I must do my best to rectify that situation as soon as possible.

Well in the words of the poets I'm "plumb tuckered out." So as soon as I can think of a finish line I'll close (this may go on for pages). It was wonderful talking to you the other night. As I think back over it you *did* sound a little more peppy than formerly—and at 2 a.m. too. Tell me more about your new personality. Hey Jo, hey? And that means write me soon. Take care and let's make some more records together someday before we're both too old to care what they sound like. Wish you were here for Stokowski. But then you have Peter van Steeden back there. So you should care, and I do.

Love,
Stanislaus

July 20, 1945
My Dearest Huckleberry,

For once I can't think of anything to write to you. Seems like nothing has happened to me since I wrote you last except I've lost two more pounds and that can't be too exciting for you.

Two times last week I got telegrams which turned out to be from various organizations around town who just sure would like me to sing for them. Each time I held my breath because I was just sure they were from you telling me what train you were arriving on. I have news for you, neither of them said anything of the kind. I'm telling you Paul, it's hard on my poor little jangled nerves. Aren't you coming? Hey baby, heh? The Prez didn't say anything about my albums while he was here, except in a jocular way. I told him I was getting a little unhappy on account of it had been [sic] so long in the offing and everybody except Fowler and Wolf were making albums. He just said it was because I had been back here so long and you were out there. I was scared to say anything more about you coming here. I had already nagged them ragged about that. So I just decided to shut up about it. He also reminded me that I was getting more regular releases than anyone else and he thought perhaps that was more important at present. I've found that sometimes it's unwise to press him too far on a subject. He just becomes stubborn if you do. The best way is the "well, you're the boss and whatever you say goes," and then look resigned and sad. He can't stand that very long. The only catch is I can't work that on him except in person. So you can see what a dilemma I'm in. Why don't you see what you can do out there. He's right in that I have been getting good releases. But I am selfish I am, and I'd like to have an album out. And besides I'd like to neck with my conductor and arranger. And I don't mean Robert Russell Bennett. Do you think I sound more peppy Paul?

Tell me how your personal appearance on Al "Pops" Jarvis' radio show turned out? Are you and Dex still on speaking terms? Or did that do it? Also, who were the other musical minds?

While I think of it. Are you following Dick Tracy? If you are, don't you think it would have been wonderful when the old farmer plowed Breathless under if he'd said "Plant you now, dig you later."

I'm gonna have my picture on the front of one of Capitol's songs. I'm doing "Gee, it's Good to Hold You" on a Chesterfield show August 2nd. So I'll be introducing it and Mickey and Dave said they'd put my picture on the cover.

Have you had your tonsils out yet? And just what is supposed to take place if you don't have them out? Do you curl up and die at any set date or what? As you walk down the path of life Paul, there are bigger things than tonsils you'll find. Of course I haven't seen your tonsils, but I still don't see…oh well.

Dave, Chris, Mickey, and I made a cozy foursome at Woody Herman's opening last Monday night.[124] We had a good time. Mickey is very funny I think. The things he says reminds me of you. He was telling us of a horrible thing that happened to him. His wife invited some people over to their house—Mick didn't know them—(anyway) [and] the man turned out to be Arthur Murray's brother. When he found out that Mickey didn't know how to rumba he was insistent that Mickey allow him to teach him then and there. The fact that Mickey didn't want to learn and the record player was broken made no difference to this eager beaver. He said every man should know how—and they could hum couldn't they. Anyway, Mickey got awfully embarrassed and had a terrible time putting the guy off. He finally just had to say no and look sorta menacing at the man. Chris and I laughed all our mascara off. He reacts to things just exactly like you do. I told him about you and Axe [sic] on the boat. Hey, would you take me on the boat sometime? I promise I'll say below instead of downstairs and all that stuff. I could learn to "battin' down the hatches" in no time.

I saw Billy Butterfield the other day. He'd just come from his draft board. He had his physical, passed, and had already been sworn in. He didn't look too happy. I can't blame him. Poor guy, he has the usual two weeks before he leaves for camp.

Mike made what might be a good suggestion for the record company the other day. He thinks you all should look into the Ziggy Elman situation. Zig may be out of the army soon and Mike thinks you should sign him up right now. I wanted to tell you about it and I'm also gonna write John. Mike talked to Ziggy's lawyers the other day and told them Capitol was a good place for him and said they seemed to like the idea. The man to contact on the coast is Artie Michaud. I think Zig is a good commercial musician. What do you think of the idea?

Mike has finally found what he thinks is a good idea for a show for me. He hasn't told me much about it, but he seems to think it's very good. We may make a wax of it in a couple of weeks. It has to be written up. We'll use my records and dub them in for the music. The only catch is it would be an expensive show. It involves guest stars, but big ones that cost money. So it'll require a big budget. Mike says if we can swing it, it should be terrific. He's been awfully particular about ideas for a show of my own. He thinks it'd be smarter to stay where I am than go on with something that might lay a bomb in thirteen weeks. He seems to have a lot of confidence in this latest one though. So hold your breath.

Maybe it's just as well that I wasn't there for that first Stokowski concert. I'm sure I'd have caused some kind of a spectacle. That Tchaikovsky *Sixth* is just about my favorite. And I've been known to act up pretty awful at *Tristan und Isolde* in that love death or whatever you call it. You'd probably have gotten embarrassed at me. Gosh, I bet it was wonderful. I've never been to a concert at the [Hollywood] Bowl. I think that should be real hot. So that's another place you've gotta take me.

I've got to pretty up. I'm going to Madison Square Garden tonight and watch grown men beat on each other. Write me soon and please come and see me. Huh Paul?

Love,
Isolde

August 4, 1945
Darling, (new kick)

The lights have just gone out all over the world as far I'm concerned—I have to go back into the Martinique. This is my sad story. They had, as you know, another option on my services. They had to notify us before July 31st if they were going to exercise the option. I didn't worry too much about the darned thing. I didn't think they'd take it up, seeing as how there were no ropes to control the crowds on my last sensational run at that nitery. When it got to be the 25th, 26th, 27th of July I really sat back and relaxed. Everyone at G.A.C. were under the rigid instructions from Mike not to even let on that they knew me. To make a sad story sadder. On the evening of the 30th that foreigner, Dario Goldfarb, called up Tom Martin and wanted to know when they could have me for my return engagement.[125] Well sir, you can just imagine how I received this perfectly adorable bit of news. I quit the business entirely and was on my way home inside of thirty seconds over a sirloin. I was eating steak when informed—sort of a last supper effect. Mike listened to me rant and rave for fifteen minutes, then taking advantage of the fact that I was choking on a piece of steak, quietly told me to shut up and stop acting like a temperamental jerk. He has caught on to the fact that any remark of this timber staggers me into at least temporary silence. He then explained that contracts unfortunately were contracts. That he would do the best he could about cutting down the shows, and the length of my stay, but I would either have to put in an appearance or drop dead. When I thought of the Martinique I took quite a fancy to the latter suggestion. To date he has been able to talk them out of me doing the late show. I'll just do the dinner and midnight [shows]. And besides all that Crosby is older and Frankie is bolder and the Martinique is really an opium den and Polly Adler's headquarters.[126] One other item, Mike says he could probably postpone the thing for a year if I wanted him to, but he suggests doing it and getting it over with so I can forget it once and for all. On that point I agree. It certainly won't seem right being there and not seeing you walk in long about twelve o'clock. Now that I think of it, it won't seem right being there...

Bullets is in town. He now has civilian clothes on and is really livin' a mile a minute. Andy Russell, the Mexican, is screaming his little curly head off about Sam Steifel, the answer to show business.[127] As a manager that guy lays bigger bombs than B-29s. And now that he is out of the army Mike wants a different deal between the two of them. As long as Bullets was in the army Mike wouldn't do anything, but now he can't see why he should do all the work and have Bullets collecting as much as he does. They have a half-and-half agreement. While I grew gray hair he offered to give me back to Bullets bag and baggage rather than continue with the present set-up. Bullets was very nice about it and agreed that Mike didn't have a fair deal. The two of us had a long talk in which he wanted to know how I felt about it. I told him they'd have to settle the thing themselves. I wasn't gonna be put on the spot of having to say I choose your style. I did tell him that I wouldn't be willing to stay back here and buck this town without Mike to help me. If he went out of the picture I'd just go home and take life easy. I can always make a living. I assured him that if that did happen to feel perfectly all right about it because I'd be just as happy, maybe happier. Fame and fortune still holds no particular thrill for me. I told him that I was very fond of Mike, but I was also very fond of him and I would never do anything to hurt him or [do anything] that he thought was unfair. I think that made him feel better. He's a pretty sentimental little guy about a lot of things. I think the way it'll end up is with Bullets getting 2.5% and Mike 7.5%. It'll be better that way. It really wouldn't be fair for Bullets to get the same as Mike and not do a darn thing. I don't feel too badly about it. When you get right down to it Bullets never really did anything towards actually helping my career anyway. What he did do he has been amply paid for. Mike got me after I had a pretty good start too. But now he is really valuable and has proved it many times in the last few months. I've told the both that as far as who gets the credit for what success I've enjoyed there is only one and his name is Prez. So much for the darker side of my life.

I hope the Davis show turns out better than you seem to think it will. It'll be all right. Andy is a good singer and you do some nice things with him. You're always too pessimistic about everything and you're gonna disillusion me yet. On September 3rd I shall be sitting in front of my radio listening and probably crying out my eyes because my boy is making beautiful music for someone else. But I'll listen, I will.

How come you're thinner? Are you dieting? I'm at a standstill—can't seem to get below 145. I still think we're gonna have to blast to get me any lower.

I wish I could see your pretty little bedroom with its pretty new little furniture. Speaking of your bedroom brings to mind a question I've been meaning to ask you for some time. On my last trip home—at your request—you became the owner of an 8x10 photo of me, which you said you were going to put on that chest of drawers in your room. Now what I want to know is this. Is it on the chest or is it in a drawer shuffled up with that batch of pictures of various "Yankee girls" that I saw? If the latter be true I would appreciate it if you'd remove same and promptly tear to shreds. The least you could do would be to put it with some old Rudy Vallée arrangement. It'd feel more at home.

Speaking of pictures I've just had a whole new bunch made and I won't feel right—and neither will Chris—until you've passed and analyzed them. Here is my plan; as soon as I get the prints of all of them I'll send you one of each. In the lower right hand corner they'll be numbered. I'll have an identical numbered batch here; you study them and let me know what you think by mail with the corresponding number before each analyzation. I think the above scheme is very clever of me and hope you do too.

I'm glad you agree with me about that chord of Robert Russell Bennett's arrangement of "Boy Next Door." Remember I told you about it the first time I did the song on that show? Isn't it revolting? You're lucky in that his novelty arrangements can bring you back to normal. They just make me hysterical. I'm doing "Dream" tomorrow at sort of a fox trot tempo. I asked the arranger to use the chorus on account of that's such a good harmony piece. I guess he thought he'd surprise me by using a quartet instead of the whole group. He knows I know The Pied Pipers. What's the use in saying anything, you'll hear it.

I'm an orphan this weekend. Chris, Ruck, and Pauline went to the country, so I'm just sitting here feeling sorry for myself and imagining what a pitiful picture I must make.

Did you hear me on the Chesterfield show last Thursday? Johnnie Johnston is on now, taking Perry's place while he's in California. John is a dear, dear boy—also a big jerk. He at least is letting his hair grow back to its original color. It's sort of startling at present.

You told me that you had written a new song but you forgot to tell me the name of it and it would be a handy thing to know—if you don't mind old boy. And if Ella Mae comes out with a record of it, [or] anyone else for that matter, I shall quit the "business" and join Polly Adler's club for girls and you'll never hear of me again.

Don't feel too badly about Hutton. Always remember there are other fish in the ocean, as we sometimes say, or to put it in still another way, other pebbles on the beach. If at this point you have an inclination to say, "fish and pebbles to you," just control your frazzled nerves and remember, time heals all things, except athlete's foot, of which I have a severe case of at the moment. Some people might say, "and what has Betty Hutton got to do with athlete's foot?" I, however, have no trouble in knowing that somehow, somewhere there is a definite resemblance. Besides there's always Anita O'Day.

I've been down several times to hear Woody Herman's band. Boy what an orchestra. I could listen to them every night. I'd probably embarrass you if you ever took me though. I'm very liable to bounce in rhythm, snap my fingers, and yell "Ow!" occasionally. You don't like that sort of thing, do you Paul?

I hope that the Ziggy [Elman] thing works out all right. Mike really deserves the credit though. I wouldn't have known about it except through him. And it was his idea for me to tell you all about it.

Please take note that I answered your letter practically immediately. I desperately hope you'll do the same. I couldn't possibly tell you how disappointed I am that you won't get to come back here. There is a plot afoot, there's got to be. I'm gonna come home as soon as I can. Even if I can just stay a short while—heaven knows when that'll be. One comfort is, it's got to be sometime (I've got clothes and car out there). Write me soon love bug.

xxxxxxxxx
oooooooooo,
Pamela

> I hope that the Ziggy thing works out all right, Mike really deserves the credit though, I wouldn't have known about it except through him, and it was his idea for me to tell you all about it.
>
> Please take note that I answered your letter practically immediately, I desperately hope you'll do the same, I couldn't possibly tell you how disappointed I am that you wont get to come back here, there is a plot afoot, there's got to be, I'm gonna come home as soon as I can, even if I can just stay a short while, heaven knows when that'll be, one comfort is, its got to be sometime, I've got clothes and car out there. Write me soon love-bug—
>
> XXXX XXXXXXXXXXX XXXXX XXX
> OOOOO OOO OO OOOOOO
> XX XXXXX XX XXXXX XXXXXX
> OO O OO OO OO O O OOOO OO
> XXXXXX XXXX XXXXXXXXXXX
> OOO OO OOO OO OO OOOO
> XXX XX XX XX XX XX XXXXX
> OO O OO OO OOOO OO OO
> XXXX XXXX XXXXXX XXXXX
> OO OOO O O OOOO OOO
> XXX XXX XX X XXXXX XXX
> OO OO OO O OO OOOO
> XXX XXX XXX XXXXXXXXX
> OO OO OO OOOO OOO O
> XXX XX XX XX XXXXXXX X,
>   *Pamela*

Jo Stafford's closing on letter dated August 4, 1945. Courtesy of Amy Weston.

Dearest Jo Ann,

Rumors concerning you are just flitting all over town; and only the Jap surrender is giving you any competition at all. Every time I see Frank [Sinatra] he tells me you're just about set on the show. Everyone here—including the Prez—thinks it would be fine; but I suppose between the Martinique, *Ford Show*, and the financial angle there's plenty to consider. Then in from N.Y. comes Al Levy with all sorts of exciting tales about your romantic situation.[129] Axel tells me it's serious as hell and that you may get married; Frank shook his head and said, "Yes it sure is serious." Al comes up with more fantastic stories of catch-as-catch-can love-making in public places. And the Prez and I have decided that you and June should have a double wedding out here as soon as possible.[130] June has found someone she's even more crazy about than "King" Cole. So if [Hedda] Hopper can make it we could stage the mass wedding of the century. I've sent my tuxedo to the cleaners and I'll be all set provided I don't have to have my tonsils out that day. The only sort of tragic note in the whole setup is the fact that I received a letter from a fan today saying that you and I could make beautiful music together. Of course it's nothing but Kismet, that's what it is. But then who are we to interfere in what the gods have decreed. Enough for my aching heart, except that in answer to your question of where that picture is. I hate to have to admit it's on my bureau. In view of present developments I now flip a coin each morning to see if I should put it in the drawer; and so far you've won every morning. But who can tell—tomorrow maybe?

I think the Mike/Bullets thing worked out very well. I certainly agree that Mike deserves the major part of the credit—except as you say for the Prez—and it would be pretty rough for you to go it with George handling the whole thing. Steifel is just about the funniest man in town these days, with the possible exception of Ken Dolan. John has been entertaining his brother from Savannah, who confided to Conkling that he guessed John was "doing pretty well for himself out here."[131] He didn't know John wrote "Dream" and really has no conception of what John is really doing. John and Harold are very busy with their show and we don't see too much of him;[132] but he's been in good moods lately and we've had a hell of a lot of laughs. I'm right in the middle of the O'Brien music—expect to record it this Friday. And then when Louis Butler's album is finished I may get my tonsils out (big laugh all over town); the Pipers are [also] beginning to scream for an album. But I want you to remember, if you get out here on that Sinatra show, we'll finish your album even if we have to do it at Music City with me on the piano.

I am going thru physical torture to bring this little missive to you because at present I possess two "charley horses" and a sprained finger on my right hand. I've been athletic as all hell playing baseball the last two Saturdays and it finally caught up with me. Everyone got banged up. Frank has one bad leg and yelled so much he could hardly sing in the Bowl. Last Sunday we all went sailing and Frank pulled a real Frank Merriwell rescue of a kid who fell off a pier—went right in and pulled him out.[133] It looked a little rough for a minute when the kid's father jumped in on top of both of them but it turned out OK.

The new song we wrote is called "Day by Day" and Frank is making it on his next date.[134] I guess some one of his firms in N.Y. will get a copy to you. They won't work on it for a while, so there's plenty of time.

I earnestly await your pictures. And if there are any in bridal costume, just send them along with the rest. I'm a good loser and I'll judge them all with the same intense scrutiny and careful consideration that I employed in New York—under shall we say more happy circumstances. I'm throwing myself into my work these days trying to forget. And if suddenly I don't hear from you anymore I'll certainly understand. Of course I'll hit you right over your peppy skinny empty head, but I'll understand. As Mama Hutton said under similar circumstances, "Tell Me All Caldonia."

Seriously, take it easy and write real soon.

Love,
Clement

August 19, 1945
Dearest Baby-Doll Darling Clement,

Happy rumor to you, and also happy V-J Day to you. I am going to start off this letter in a long lengthy talk on how the only person who can really know the truth in a situation is the person who finds himself in that particular situation. I shall tell you the whole story from beginning to end, and trust it will go no farther than your little Phi Beta Kappa mind. This will no doubt be a big mistake on my part, but I've been making them all my life so one more won't hurt anything, except me. To begin with, there are two men in my life who interest me—in shall we say the romance department: one being Mike Nidorf; the other being a musician by the name of Paul Weston—that isn't his real name, but that's unimportant.

I've known Paul for a long time, but existing circumstances and blondes just weren't conducive towards our relationship being anything but the blood buddy sort of thing. Last winter Paul came East and we saw a lot of each other—still on the buddy kick—until one night he kissed me and I thought why, oh why, didn't someone hit either him or me on the head a long time ago. Anyway, as far as I was concerned it was a real nice surprise—that kiss. After that a lot more real nice surprises occurred. Such as getting pleasantly excited when I was going to be with him and remaining in the same state when I was with him.

Then he had to go back to California. Before long I followed and enjoyed myself with him out there about as thoroughly as I've ever enjoyed myself with anyone. However the visit was short and before I knew it I was back in N.Y.C. Then Mike came on the scene. Not being one who likes to stay in her room and look out the window, especially when there is no particular reason for doing so, I saw and am still seeing a lot of Mike, who is one of the nicest, kindest, and most considerate men I've ever met. Now

I won't go into my life with men in the past, but I'll tell you I was never used to such wonderful treatment from them before. He treats me like the Queen of May and I take to it like a duck takes to water, or a cat having its back scratched. It's nice to be treated like a lady instead of Bridget the maid.[135] I may be wrong, but I'm only human. I think the reason for all the marriage rumors is because we are seen together so much. Mike, of course, has taken out many girls in the past, but I don't think he ever was really serious about any of them. He is about me and makes no bones about it to anyone who cares to listen. I can't go around making speeches about how my mind is far from being made up so people just come to the wrong conclusions and I can't help it. However Mike knows it isn't and that's the most important thing. I think he knows the reason too, having made such remarks as, "That Weston is a hell of a nice guy and I like him very much. But I wish he was 80,000 miles or so farther away." I think he knows that as far as I'm concerned you are no longer just my favorite conductor.

Well sir, that's the situation as it now stands. As I said before, this is probably a big mistake to tell you all these things. It says in books on "how to snare unsuspecting men" that you are supposed to be coy about such things. But I don't know how to be coy, so I'm a dead duck. Now you can go out and have a big laugh on me and take another starlet out. But you can never say I didn't tell you the whole truth, and nothing but the truth. So there.

We did a very dull show today. This was a day of national prayer and if our listeners had any brains at all they shut their radios off and did their praying while we were on. Robert Russell is simply chocked full of novel ideas and by gad we do 'em right over the wireless and cover all the forty-eight to boot.

I saw a new musical called *Marinka* the other night and it was up to the usual NY musical standards[136]—it stunk in ten different keys. Honestly, Charlie Wick could do as well, and you'll have to admit that's saying a mouthful.

I got a letter from John Hud the other day. He couldn't say where he was, but I take it he's on some island in the Pacific. Anyway, he was talking about going swimming in these wonderful coves, crystal clear water and coral reefs, etc.—and you know that ain't Catalina [Island]. He sounds like his usual zany self. To quote part of his letter he said, "We are all brown as nuts. Some of us are even brown as Indians. I hope none of us get as black as the ace of spades." He has a great brain. I called his mother the night peace was declared and she certainly sounded happy.

I hope your poor little charley horses and your poor little sprained finger on your right hand got well all right. I guess we just aren't the athletic type. Huh Paul? Every time I get outdoor-ish something terrible happens and I'm concentrating on Gin Rummy. I did get daring last Monday though. Larry Brooks and I went to Coney Island and went on everything. Jeekers some of those rides are scary. And I just yelled for three solid hours. It was fun though—sort of.

They start to work on the Chesterfield contracts tomorrow. I've told Mike and Rockwell that I won't sign unless they call for a certain amount of time in California each year. They don't seem to think there will be any trouble on that score. Gee, I just wish and wish that you were gonna be on with me. I don't care what anyone says, I'm not singing as good as I used to with you. I just simply can't sing with these old pukey arrangements they give me. There isn't any inspiration at all—and I sure get plenty brought sometimes.[137] Oh boy how I'd like to sing with you back of me again. I can't begin to tell you how much I miss that. They way it stands now I'll get to before long. I told Mike that I wanted to go home to make my records for the album. They'll be better if I make them with you conducting Paul. I'm sure going to try to get out there. I finish at the club on the 23rd of October and we'd come out as soon after that as possible. I'll have to be back here about the 1st of December. If I do come I'll probably knock your eyes out on account of I got some spiffy new clothes the other day. A couple of them were size fourteen. As the Prez would say, "Gott Dogg!"

I haven't got all my new pictures yet, but as soon as I get them I'll send them on. Also, I'll send you a list of tunes in the next couple days. If you and John don't like any of them just say so, because I trust you and your taste more than my own.

It was wonderful to talk to you the other night—as it says in the song, "Why Don't We Do This More Often?"[138] Hey, I gotta get dressed now. Write soon. I did what you said about "telling all Caldonia." So I expect the same from you. I'll probably just go on expecting, however, because as I said long ago you are the cagey type and also the beating-around-the-bush sort. And I'm not very clever at "reading between the lines." And that's [the] how darkies were born blues.

Love,
Stella Dallas[139]

[September 1, 1945][140]
Dearest Jo-Ann Honey Darling Sweetie,

Here I sit attempting to compose funny sounding music, which will sound as funny as the jokes all the comical people will say on the radio Monday night. Or at least as funny as Andy Russell when he's singing in Mexican. However, contrary to all expectation, the show looks like fun. [It is] little work and everyone seems to get along pretty well—if you don't count Sam Steifel and me.

Bonnie called me yesterday and said she'd had a letter from you or Chris saying you definitely were not coming back in October because Mike thought you'd lose too much money.[141] I presume he knows what's best for you. But I can't see why your tax problem is any different from anyone else's; and as long as the law hasn't changed I still think there's a limit to the amount of money you can make. I'm also certain that the only way you'll get your album made is to come out here and make it. And that would not only seem to be a sizeable source of revenue, but more than that it would do you more good than thirty Ford shows or sixty Chesterfield. Or am I bitter? We would much prefer to have you make your next release out here, even if we have to hold up the whole release a few days in waiting for you to get here to record.

Incidentally, on the "Day by Day" routine the following has happened. Now you know how I love talking about my own songs, etc., but through Sinatra "Bullets" heard about the song and Andy wants to do it. I told him you had first call on it. And since then the Pipers have asked for it, saying "Jo has all the good tunes" blues. Well I told them all you had first shot at it if you wanted it. So if you decide you aren't interested—and I wouldn't blame you after this confused paragraph—just let me know and we can let the Pipers and Andy fight it out. We figure your next record release for December 1 and that's why we'd like to do it here as soon as you finish at the Martinique. And if I tell Glenn you're not coming back he'll sure "snap his cap." [That's a] hot expression heard in the Key Club. I think Don Raye said it.

The sensation of the past few weeks is the approaching Sammy Cahn wedding, which will shake Hollywood's social foundations like they've never been shocked before. It will be in the Gold Room of the Hotel Ambassador and it should be quite a brawl. Axel is to be best man; and the sight of Axel that close to a wedding ceremony is at least worth the price of admission. What am I talking about? The question of who is to be invited, etc. is discussed on every street corner and I think all will be glad when next Wednesday comes and the whole thing is over with.

Finally am all finished with the Margaret O'Brien deal. Metro [Goldwyn Mayer] approved the whole thing and were very complimentary about the music, which makes me quite gay. I never did anything like that before and was pretty scared about how it would turn out. The Prez is quite his usual self these days. He comes in the office and we all go off to lunch in strange places like the Farmer's Market. All-in-all things are quite pleasant.

I certainly was most interested in your *long lengthy talk*, which was contained in your last letter. I can't agree with your beliefs that frankness doesn't pay and that coyness is the best approach for men over thirty. I must admit that the gentle considerate treatment is employed by all too few males and it would be a hell of a good thing to have a revival of chivalry in the next few years. I guess I just never could get with it. I almost get nauseous when I have to walk around a car to open a door for a girl; and when it comes to having to go and get people to bring them to your house to dinner I just up and revolt. In short I am quite a bit of a jerk, seeing as how I think if women want to vote they can open their own car doors too. And I know I'm wrong as hell and I really don't believe what I'm writing, but I sound so forward and brave saying it. The above statements probably have you much annoyed at me; and I can hear you thinking, "There he goes evading again" and "the hell with him Jack." But when you've been beating around the bush so busily and blindly for ten years it's hard to reverse and sit down and rest for a while; and we'll have to get loaded and have a nice long talk about everything as soon as you get here and I repeat *get here*. And you are going to get here, aren't you, hey Jo Ann, hey?

I'm definitely not going to read that last paragraph over. I feel like I just took a very mediocre chorus on "Dinah" in Ab and the leader has just said, "From now on you stick to ballads, Meyer." He thinks I won't practice; but I will. And I'll show him someday.

Little George Durgom got tears all down the front of my suit the other night concerning the Jo Stafford situation. I played so dumb that I even said, "I thought no one in the world should have a dime of her record royalties as no-one got her the job." That hit the little fellow right between the eyes, but he rallied. And I must admit it tugs at one's heartstrings a little to hear his side of the tale. He's not at all bitter at you and realizes that with him as your sole manager you wouldn't mean a thing. But he just seems to think he should get something and it's completely immaterial to me what the hell happens as long as you're happy with the situation. I sure would like to be able to talk with you for about six hours about the whole set-up: records, managers, Martinique, romance, marriage, Hughie Prince, Catalina, your piano, vocal arrangements, Palladium openings, movies at the Esquire, and Mr. Few.[142] That's enough, because you know how the Prez hates those songs where you list things.

Write soon Jo and please plan on coming out. The Capitol setup is worth more than a few hundred clams and I hate to see that album fading back into oblivion. It would be wonderful for you, so come on out and let's get the damn thing finished. Take care and don't let people talk you out of things.

Love,
Sigmund Spaeth[143]

September 16, 1945
Dearest Paulecito querido mio,

I've just finished reading *The Captain from Castile* and now have a violent crush on Pedro De Vargas, hero of same. Just thought I'd explain so you wouldn't be upset if I should so happen to toss off a Spanish phrase or two.

Do you know that I came near starting this letter off with an apology about waiting so long to answer? Then I recalled how many times I'd waited for you and thought better of it. Just lost my head for a few minutes.

Well sir, I'm down there at that place again.[144] Opened last Wednesday night with the usual hysteria that always accompanies my openings. I hate opening days. I'd rather eat old, rusty tacks any day. It's much better this time—a lot more folks seem to know who I am. Also not having to do that late show is a lifesaver.[145] I open with "Sunny Side," then "Only Have Eyes for You, Baby."[146] And I'm doing a tune of Matt Dennis' ("I Almost Did But I Didn't"). It's a "I Said No, He Said Yes" thing in which I sort of roll my eyes and look suggestive. I close with "A.T. & S."[147] Now for the killer. I come back then and tell stories with Lou Holtz.[148] The kind of stuff that Wen used to do with Junie. Then I do a song with him ("Delightful, Delicious, Delovely"). All he does is say "It's every time, it seems to go all right." This'll kill you. All the comments on opening night were that I saved Holtz' act with the bit I did with him. I thought you and John would like that.

I hear that the Prez will be in before the end of the month. Is that true or can I expect an answer from you by the end of the month? If he does come in I'll still be at the club and he'll come and see me and I'll just simply die from nervous fits. He's never seen me perform in public. I'll probably be so scared if he comes down that I'll stink it up something awful and it'll be real terrible.

Pauline and Christine left for Tennessee and Gibson Holler yesterday morning[149]—they flew down. If you see anybody from home don't say anything about them flying. It might get back to Mama and she'd just naturally blow her top. They haven't been back there since before I was born; which shall we say is closer to twenty eight years than twenty seven. The family left there just two months before the arrival of the future chanteuse of the La Martinique, swank nitery of Manhattan (as it says in the papers). They'll be seeing our Grandmother for the first time in eleven years. She's certainly excited about them coming down. And here I am, all by myself, fighting off the ghosties and spookies every night. I guess they'll have a good time. Seeing a lot of relatives they haven't seen in so many years. 'Course the fact that only a couple of houses have inside plumbing may give them food for thought now and then. But that's life. Or should I say, that's Gibson Holler.

The Chesterfield contract has finally been signed. They were very nice about giving us stuff that we wanted. Mike got them to just make it for a year—and in twenty-six periods instead of thirteen. Also at the end of the first twenty-six they have to let me off for six weeks so I can come home. The thing I like best is the year deal. At first they had their usual eighty years with options. Not that they'd keep me that long anyway, but it's nice to know that when a year is up they won't have any contract to hold me to. If you were back here you could have the conductor spot as easy as jumping off a log. They still don't know who we're gonna have. It also says in the contract that I have to okay the conductor. I don't know anyone back here to okay except maybe Pee Wee Russell—and I think he's tied up down at Nick's. I start December 11th. Or did I already tell you that?

I saw Billy Wilson today.[150] He said to send you his regards. Here's one. He's the producer on the R.C.A. show—with you know who as the M.C. Eh law, tempus does fugit by, it really do.

We've got our plane tickets for home already. As scared as I am of flying, I couldn't stand that train trip again this year. Now all we have to do is keep Mama from finding out how we're coming. We leave on the 25th of October at noon. So we'll arrive at—as my Aunt Lizzie says—"some ungotly hour" on the morning of the 26th. Oh happy day!

I'm still skinny. I only weigh 137 now. I'm getting sort of scared now because I'm not dieting very seriously and I still seem to go on losing. I guess as long as I feel good everything is all right. My Mama is just gonna beat on me when she sees me though. Gee it sounds good to say Mama. Sometimes I just sit and say it over and over in my mind. When I get home I'm just gonna sit and look at her for a couple of days. Guess that's sort of silly at age twenty seven, huh?

Well, I finally heard from Bullets. And he informed me that he just simply loved me to death, but he wasn't giving an inch on the contract. So he's now sitting out there on his rusty dusty collecting the same as Mike—not that he ever did anything to collect for. But it really stinks now. It takes me a long time to get mad at people, but when I do there isn't any changing my mind. I put up with him for a long time without opening my mouth about anything to anyone—and paid off regularly for nothing. He's really torn his pants with me this time—and if you'll excuse me for a minute—he can go straight to hell. I hope he chokes with the money he gets. I don't pretend to be very intelligent, but I have got good horse sense. I'm usually pretty fair minded about things—and as far as I'm concerned this really reeks. He was pretty stupid in his letter too by inferring some bad things about Mike, which true or false, have no bearing on the case. All I know is what Mike has done so far as my manager. And may I say that Bullets' performances in the past in that capacity don't stack up very well in comparison. I've made up my mind not to say a word about it to him when I'm out there. All I hope is he doesn't come around and want to be blood buddies. He's liable to end up with no hair at all. Please don't say anything about this to anyone. Please Paul? And don't forget and confide in the Prez. He's got to end up behind the eight ball doing stuff like this. But it won't be because I've said anything. Let him ruin himself.[151]

Well, now that I've blown my top completely, it's time for me to go to bed. It's way late in the morning and I'm freezing to death. Write me soon and I'll answer quicker if you do. By the way, I won Martin Block's poll again—by 20,000 votes this time.[152] Gee I wish I could win Martin.

                Love,
                Cantana
                In the book De Vargas loves Cantana.

Arriving on the East Coast (ca. January 1945).

Dancers rehearse for the La Martinique floor show.

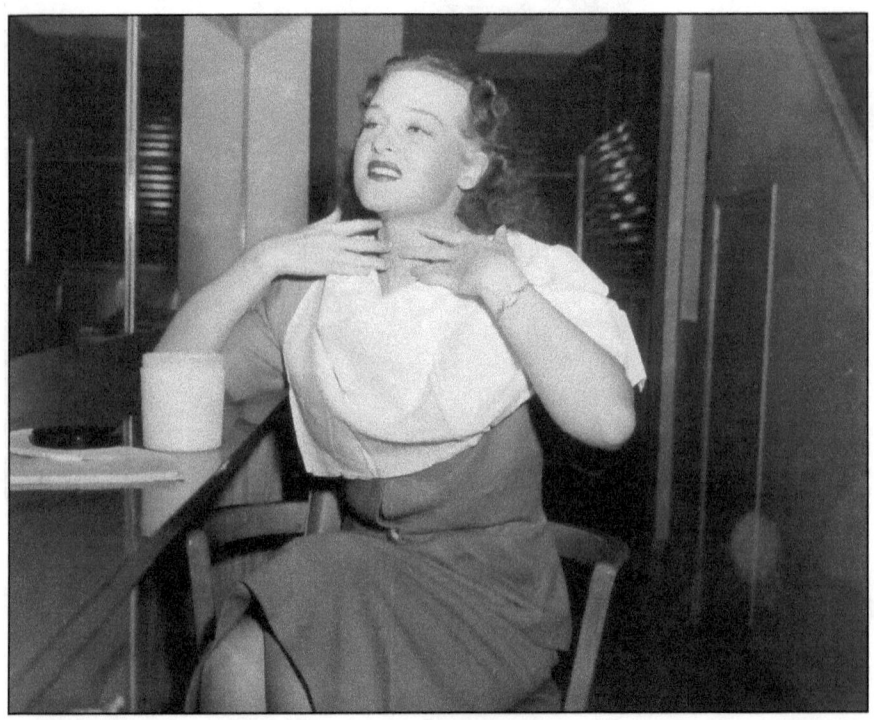
Getting ready for a performance (1945).

J. S. and band leader Carl Ravazza at the La Martinique.

Frank Sinatra makes an appearance during Jo's opening night at the La Martinique (February 8, 1945). Band leader Carl Ravazza laughs as he stands behind the pair.

In the Paramount Theatre dressing room with band leader Charlie Spivak (seen in mirror—ca. May 1945).

Campaigning for a war relief bond (1945).

Correspondence | 149

Backstage at the Paramount Theatre with Ford Hour co-star Larry Brooks (Summer 1945).

Columnist Jill Warren and Jo's personal manager Mike Nidorf meet backstage at the Paramount Theatre (Summer 1945).

Leaving the Paramount Theatre with Mike Nidorf (Summer 1945).
There is building graffiti on Jo's right that reads, "Frank Sinatra is my boy."

Presentation of the 1945 Down Beat award for "best female vocalist" from Martin Block on the Make Believe Ballroom radio program (January 1946).

Essays by Paul Weston

Roy Harris, Record Labels, and Musical Progress

CAPITOL RECORDS, INC. AND SUBSIDIARIES
INTER-OFFICE MEMO
To: Glenn Wallichs [President], Floyd Bittaker [Vice President and General Sales Manager], Jim Conkling [Artists and Repertoire Chief], and Bob Stabler [Assistant National Sales Manager]
From: Paul Weston
Date: December 20, 1948
Subject: [Roy Harris, Record Labels, and Musical Progress]

During the past week, Mr. Roy Harris, who is considered to be one of the top six living composers in the United States today, gave a lecture at UCLA which might be of extreme importance in the future of Capitol Records, particularly as we are now taking the first steps preparatory to entering the classical field. Since the Telefunken catalogue alone is not going to be sufficient to maintain a classical library, and since our company made its initial mark in the record industry by virtue of unusual items unusually recorded, it seems that several of Mr. Harris' remarks could have a bearing on a future course of action which would pay dividends for Capitol both in a financial way and also, which might be even more important at the moment of entering a new field, in the way of prestige with the buyers of classical records whom we have never before contacted. While a great many potential buyers of our classical line are probably aware of our label through our popular records, there must be thousands of buyers to whom the term "classical records" means only Victor and Columbia, and those are the people whose attention we must attract. A good product is only half the battle, and if an opportunity for promotion presents itself, Capitol can make very good use of it.

Mr. Harris stated at UCLA that the radio and record companies have been the instruments through which music has come of age, just as the printing press enabled the written word to be made available to people all over the world. But he feels that because of a situation of which we at Capitol are well aware, the American public is not being kept abreast of what is going on in the musical world today. Mr. Harris is very outspoken—he speaks of "those two big cartels"—CBS and NBC that have almost complete control over the live and recorded music that is being heard in the country today. Now this is no idle talk. The control of CBS over the New York Philharmonic and of NBC over the NBC Symphony is pretty well known to all, and as was mentioned above, to most record buyers of the classical line there are only two companies, Victor and Columbia (both of which are controlled by NBC and CBS). Mr. Harris states that the reason that more contemporary compositions are not recorded is the matter of royalties which have to be paid to present day composers while the music of the masters is royalty free. This argument shouldn't make sense permanently, since it would mean that no new music will ever be recorded again. If Mr. Harris is offered the opportunity of getting a new work recorded, the chances are that he or any other living composer would be only happy to make a deal which would distribute the royalty load fairly for both record company and composer.

In his lecture, Mr. Harris gave as his first requisite for the successful development of music in this country an "honest to God" record company, which would take the lead in attempting to develop some musical progress. Now no one needs to be reminded that no record company is going to take the chance of being "honest to God," as Mr. Harris puts it, unless there's a chance for it to make a little profit on the deal. But the trouble with the situation might just happen to be that fact that Columbia and Victor are just as lazy and slack in adopting progressive methods in classical recording as they have been in the popular field. No one wanted to take a chance on recording a lot of things until Capitol took the lead in the popular field—special material, different types of artists, children's records as a major project—all of these and many more were neglected by self-satisfied recording men of the bigger companies, and along came Capitol and made use of their deficiencies. Mr. Harris says that the record companies are the "bottleneck" in the path of musical progress in the classical field. But the record companies he's talking about are Victor and Columbia, and there's no more reason why Capitol should follow their techniques than there was in the popular field. We have the Telefunken catalogue to compete with their "many times over" recorded music of the masters. But somewhere in this country there must be a market for some new music, and Capitol can be just the company to bring it to the market. In popular recording you can no longer get away with just having an artist sing a chorus and a half of a song just as it was written. The public now expects more: an arrangement that entertains them and a routine that's somewhat out of the ordinary. In many ways Capitol took the lead in bringing about this change, and there's no reason why it cannot assume an attitude of leadership upon its entry into the classical field.

In its more progressive days, Victor was looked to by the composers of America for leadership and help in getting American music performed and recorded. Prizes were offered and records were made of the winning compositions. This has been under discussion at Capitol for some time, and it would seem that now might be the time for some action. The cost is very small when one realizes the gains which can be made prestige-wise. One of the reasons Victor held the leadership in the classical field was that she assumed it, and there's no reason why it couldn't be taken away from her if she's unwilling to continue work towards her original objectives. At least three of the top six composers in the country are in Los Angeles this week, and if a move could be made to invite these men into a discussion in which they would make suggestions for a completely new approach to the recording of classical contemporary music in the country, the advantages to Capitol in promotion and prestige would be difficult to overestimate. Supposing that in his lectures throughout the country Mr. Harris, instead of confining himself to damning Columbia and Victor, would be boosting Capitol as the new progressive force in American music. Supposing Mr. Copland, in his recitals and talks, would mention that he had been consulted by Capitol to advise them as to the best methods of once again stirring interest in young American composers. All the music which is to be recorded in the classical field hasn't yet been written. And why shouldn't Capitol assume the post of leader in this field, as she has in popular music? If these two men, who command thousands of lines of newspaper space each year throughout the country could be made Capitol boosters in addition to being critical of Columbia and Victor, then Capitol can develop a whole new market not only for its Telefunken line, but for its popular records too. Everything we have on Telefunken has been well recorded over and over on those two labels, and only quality and prestige will enable us to outsell them. Here's a chance to get more prestige.

The Hit Psychology

July 30, 1949

Throughout the past four of five years, a mental attitude has been building up among record people that seems to be based on a completely false premise, yet it has become so prevalent that it now exists on every level of the record industry, from the top executives right through to the salesmen. This is the "hit" psychology, the belief that the only way to save the record business is through "hits." Now in this connection a statement of one of our biggest motion picture men is quoted, namely "There's nothing wrong with business that a good picture won't cure." This is applied to the record business in saying, "There's nothing wrong with the record business that a hit record won't cure." But there's a tremendous difference in the two adjectives. Notice that the movie executive said "good," not "hit." The failure to ignore the difference between good records and hit records can be a fatal one for the record industry, since good records are not necessarily hit records—and very definitely vice versa. In the first place it might be advisable to study the "hit" phenomenon that seems so important to us, and attempt to draw some conclusions.

Very few record men in their right mind will tell you that they or anyone else can predict a hit. Many people can predict what type of tunes the American public may like, or what type of artist, tempo, arrangement, etc. However no one has yet been heralded as having the ability to predict in advance the records that will have that elusive quality which sends them up to the million mark in sales. Since each of the four major companies puts out hundreds of records a year, and seldom achieves more than two hits, the percentage is pretty small. Therefore the man who builds his business so that he must have hits to get along would almost seem to be in the gambling business rather than the record business. Since no particular individual has been able to follow with a series of successive hits, then a record man addicted to the "hit" psychology might be much better off with his company assets in the form of chips, sitting patiently beside the roulette table waiting for his favorite number to come up.

Now let's go back a few months and see if we can determine any pattern to the series of hits the record business has "enjoyed" throughout the past year. In the Billboard Disc Jockey Poll that came out October 2nd of last year, Capitol found itself in the enviable spot of having the top two records of the year, as far as hits were concerned: "Nature Boy" and "Mañana." At the very same time that the survey was published, Capitol also had the two top hits in the Billboard Retail Sellers for the week of October 2nd: "Twelfth Street Rag" and "Tree in the Meadow." Now this was pretty much a sensational spin of the wheel, as any record man will admit. However, it also could have been a dangerous turn of events in the case that the company itself started to take the top spot as a matter of course and didn't recognize the fact that as far as hits are concerned, no one has the answer. Of course, Lady Luck has long been noted for not remaining too long in any one place. In fact, she probably figured enough was enough, for on November 27, she decided that was all for "Twelfth Street Rag" and "Tree in the Meadow," because she moved in Dinah Shore with a little pop tune called "Buttons and Bows." And just to show Columbia that she could be generous, she also gave the second spot to Kay Kyser's "Slow Boat to China." "Twelfth Street Rag" hung around for a time in third place and then gave way momentarily on December 11th to a Jo Stafford and Gordon MacRae record of "My Darling." The latter never seemed to be able to make the jump into hit status. It then fell from the top three under the Christmas sales of Spike Jones' "Two Front Teeth."

Now with the start of the year the record ban was over, and another major label, which hadn't been heard from in a long time, began to make itself felt. Decca started pleasantly and quietly enough with Evelyn Knight's "Little Bird," which pushed into third place on January 1st. It disappeared for a week and then took over first place for six successive weeks, while "Buttons and Bows" and "Slow Boat" gradually subsided in favor of "Far Away Places." Margaret Whiting made the first three one week and then Crosby and Como took over—and then along came "Cruising Down the River." Blue Barron started that one, putting in his appearance on February 26th, but March 26 Decca and Russ Morgan had overtaken him. Meantime, to show that just as in the case of Capitol and Columbia, when Lady Luck smiles she practically beams. Bing Crosby slipped into third place with "Galway Bay." For a month and a half Decca had two out of the top three, although it's doubtful if at the time anyone was running around calling Crosby's "Galway Bay" a "hit." Then along came another Russ Morgan record hit, "Forever and Ever." Morgan and Blue Barron of M.G.M. held the top two spots for five successive weeks. Lady Luck would only give M.G.M. one hit, altering her "two at a time" policy, which had held sway for over a year. However, suddenly she became aware of the fact that there was one company, which she ignored shamefully, and strangely enough this was one of the largest, namely, Victor. The label hadn't even appeared for over a year in the top three of hit-dom—and it was certainly long overdue. Perry Como started by taking over third place on April 23rd, and this was with the same tune that Russ Morgan had already had in third place, "Forever and Ever." Como held down third place for three weeks and then Russ Morgan edged him out again. But up on the rail came a new entry that was to cause plenty of excitement.

Vaughn Monroe's "Riders in the Sky" jumped right into first place on May 14 and has been there ever since. It has held down the coveted spot for twelve successive weeks, which is a good showing in any league. True once more to her policy of having two at time from one company, Lady Luck has placed another Victor record in second place, Perry Como's "Some Enchanted Evening." For two months these records have been in the top three, with the third record being Gordon Jenkins' record of "Again." That record was brought into prominence by a London record, only to have Decca make a hit out of it. That's the story up to July 30 of this year.

Now in looking back over the period under consideration, certain facts do come to light. For example, Decca seems to be a past master at taking another company's hit record and turning it into one of its own. Of all the Decca hits in this period, not one was created by Decca Records. "A Little Bird" was made by Paula Watson, and Decca copied the arrangement with Evelyn Knight and turned it into a million record hit. Blue Barron had an M.G.M. hit in "Cruising Down the River" and Russ Morgan made it for Decca and turned it into a hit. Margaret Whiting had a tremendous jump on "Far Away Places," but Decca got into the top three with Crosby's record. Finally Vera Lynn made a hit record of "Again," and Decca made their own hit of "Again" by Gordon Jenkins. Now this should lay to rest for all time the big complaint about getting out first. The only company to be successful in the past six months was not first on any one of their hits. Compare this situation with that of Capitol.

Capitol's best period was during the recording ban, when it alone was able to be on the big four records. It had "Nature Boy," "Mañana,"

"Tree in the Meadow," and "Twelfth Street Rag." It might not be pleasant to speculate what might have happened had Perry Como been able to make "Nature Boy" (with orchestral background); if Evelyn Knight could have made "Mañana"; if Como or Crosby could have made "Tree in the Meadow" (the way they made "Far Away Places"); and if heaven forbid, Russ Morgan could have made "Twelfth Street Rag." That's one factor to worry about.

Capitol, the surveys show, must be alone to have a hit, while Decca thrives on competition and has made all their hits by simply recording something that has started on another label and then beating the competition's brains out. In other words, to have a hit today, Capitol would have to develop an item that Decca could not copy, and that might take some doing. "Whispering Hope" could be one of this type, but it's too early to tell.

The general conception of the word "hit" has always been something in the novelty line, something new and different. And for every new and different idea that clicks, there must be hundreds of flops. That's where the gambling element comes in. If hits are the answer, then the whole function of the repertoire department would be to look for new and different material, and put out enough releases so that percentage-wise it would have a fair chance to be lucky enough to come up with the hits. But this can't be the record business.

Over a year ago the cry was for *Hit Parade* material. In other words the songs that were the ten most popular in the country. So surveys were made and soon Capitol had a record on every one of the top ten tunes. Where formerly she had only been on two or three and had been concentrating on the novelty type of material that had brought her hits. Now it is impossible to have the cake and eat it too. Decca and Victor can do it. They have enough records per release to be able to cover pop tunes and also to try novelties. Although their hits have invariably been of the pop tune variety on which type tune Capitol cannot produce a hit record. Capitol's pop hits die a-borning, like Whiting's "Far Away Places," Stafford and MacRae's "My Darling," and Whiting and Mercer's "Baby It's Cold Outside."

The important fact to take note of is this. Capitol came into being at the time of the first Petrillo ban and rose to major status at the time of the second Petrillo ban. In other words, Capitol is in fine shape as long as it is alone by itself in the field with no competition to worry about on its "hits." Mr. Petrillo was indirectly obliging on two occasions, but he may not be again for quite some time. But during the past six months we have had a far different situation, with Decca taking the hits of other companies and making records of them which sell beyond those of the competitors who made the records hits in the first place. And what happens in the meantime?

The title "First with the Hits from Hollywood" is fine until someone asks for a definition of the word "hit." Is a hit something you must create yourself, be out first on, and then not have to worry about competition because no one else happens to be recording at the time? Then "hits" are something to be thought very well of. But when we are treated to the spectacle of the only successful company during the past six months not creating the original material, not being first on any of them, and finally actually overhauling existing competition, the original conception of a "hit" might do with a little revising. In the period under the survey above, Capitol had four hits (on all of which she was alone), Columbia had two, Decca had four, and Victor had two. On all the other majors there were competitive records available.

Now what keeps these other majors in operation when they are "between hits"? As Victor was for almost a year. The answer is just the general run-of-the-mill catalog, on which any record company should at least be prepared to break even. If hits come along that's fine, they're the gravy and the opportunity for big profit. But they only come at best twice a year. And in having four in a row (thanks to Petrillo) Capitol may have been itself guilty of starting the "hit" psychology to operate within its own organization. Hits are fine, but they're not the answer, because any record company whose mental attitude depends on sitting and waiting for those lucky breaks is doomed—at least until there's another record ban.

In closing, it might be well to quote from a Capitol branch report that shows the exact opposite of the attitude of "waiting for hits that never come in." This also points the way to the successful operation of a business where hits are delightful and well worth trying for, but are not the foundation for the successful operation of the record business.

> Let's face it, business is bad, but I am more than ever convinced that this is by far a result of lack of activity on the part of our dealers. This we must do; teach the dealer how to sell. He must realize that the greater share of the burden is to be his. We are selling him records, sure, but he is not selling them to the public. Most dealers that I have talked to are utterly free of any productive ideas regarding the merchandising of records. If this is our job then we must help him, show him, and teach him. And prove to him that his interests are our interests. For if he doesn't sell records, neither will we.

What Is Bop?

AMONG THE CURRENT PERIODICALS there is an ever-increasing tendency to publish articles attempting to define the latest musical phenomenon, bop, or be-bop, as is sometimes referred to in a usage now considered archaic by the true bopper. The whole world is divided up into two classes of people: the idols of the boppers, commonly referred to as "the greatest"; or the ordinary human beings, known as "the clowns." The chances are that you and all your friends fall into the latter category, for the system is extremely selective and there are probably only twenty or thirty people in the whole country in the first category.

There has been something of an attempt by the pioneers of bop, and particularly by the critics who write so knowingly of something they are totally unequipped to either play or understand, to make bop an affair of mystery—a sort of secret music which is incomprehensible to all but a chosen few (of their own choosing, needless to say). But all that has passed, and the poor, unenlightened American public is beginning to take to this new musical style and make it its very own, and anything which belongs to the American public is certainly no mystery. Bop will survive the stigma of darkened cellars, sly hints of oriental stimulants necessary to its full enjoyment, and the noisy and rather silly dissonances characteristic of its early stages. Lots of people who say "Oh, I can't stand that awful be-bopping music" will at that very moment be dancing gaily to a band playing bop figures on the pop tune of the day. And the use of the word "dancing" will of course cause shudders among the so-called critics, for they told us at the start the bop rhythm was supposed to be fluid, indefinite, flexible, or even non-existent.

The early musical theorists (and no matter what anyone tells you, bop is music) told us that music was composed of three elements: melody,

---

Source: Paul Weston, "What *Is* Bop?," *Musical Express*, May 13, 1949.

harmony, and rhythm. Now bop brings something new to each of these elements. To melody it brings a completely new feeling—a sort of jerky, hesitating quality which usually follows a series of rather rapidly executed musical notes. This jerky, or halting type of melody is credited by some with giving bop its name, and the story is told of Dizzy Gillespie (certainly one of "the greatest") attempting to describe his then newfound style and telling a rather amazed interviewer that he played along a while and then went "be-bop," and then started in again. Now the bop melody line is characterized by several unusual elements. For one, triplets (or notes in clusters of threes) are considered quite acceptable. In addition, the bopper is expected to make use of the most unusual notes available in the key in which he finds himself. These notes would be considered downright clinkers by someone accustomed to playing only the straight melody of any given tune. More of these notes when we come to harmony. Now this combination of unusual notes and speeded up execution probably caused more damage to bop in its early and formative stage than anything else. Anyone who could play unusual notes (in many cases downright clinkers) in a rapid disorganized fashion could call himself a bopper—and who was to say him nay. Playing very loud and very high also added to the confusion. In some cases musicians who couldn't be accepted by a leader as soloists in the conventional style found themselves a few weird notes, played fast, high, and very wrong indeed, and announced themselves as boppers—and set bop and music back a year or two.

So the contribution of bop to the element of melody in music could be summed up as a series of rather rapidly executed notes, interspersed with triplets and momentary halts, which make use of unusual and surprising melodic intervals, the end result of which has been in the past to confuse and annoy the untutored listener and to delight the true bop enthusiast tremendously. There's nothing mysterious about it, and even musicians who were rather terrified by its flashy nature at first can soon pick out the desired elements and develop their own bop style.

When we come to harmony, there is even less mystery connected with the whole thing. The basic element of bop harmony (at present) is the flatted fifth. The reason I say at present is because within a few years time the harmonic structures which seem so advanced today can become no more alarming than a simple hymn. Now lest the term flatted fifth seem mysterious, it should be explained that the fifth note from the root of the chord is dropped a half tone, which at first provided the same effect as spelling "catch" with a fifth letter not as far from the beginning of the alphabet, or spelling it "catcg." Now this would cause a little eyebrow lifting in literary circles, and the flatted fifth had the same effect on the unsuspecting musical public. And of course this flatted fifth was played as part of the melody and so brought an unusual quality to that element of music also. Now the use of these harmonic innovations made the bop enthusiasts somewhat contemptuous of the conventional harmonies, probably in much the same manner in which devotees of Wagnerian harmonies scoffed at the simple and relatively thin harmonies of Mozart. But music as a whole has a habit of surviving these little upsets, and in the end it absorbs them into itself as bop is even now being absorbed.

Finally, we arrive at rhythm, and in this element of music there has also been a great upheaval in the name of bop. The conventional contribution of the drummer in a bop band is an incessant dinning of the cymbal in order to preserve fluidity. This cymbal beat is punctuated by assorted rim shots on the side of the drum and bass drum beats, all of which fit into the pattern of the arrangement or the solo being played by the individual instrumentalist. Rhythmically, bop drummers are now playing types of beats which would have been looked upon as impossible ten years ago, just as the melodies and harmonies of bop would have been regarded at the same time. Bop demands machine-like precision from the drummer, and as time goes on the single-minded devotion to the cymbal will probably resolve itself into a more normal approach to the whole set of drums, but the precision and the rapid technique are here to stay. The orchestra as a whole is also called upon to play rhythmic figures which would have terrified musicians ten years ago, and the increased technique demanded from every member of the orchestra is a monumental contribution to music in itself.

In closing, a word about singing bop. Here the mystery deepens somewhat, for the syllables used may seem to the untutored listener to be an unknown language much too difficult to comprehend. But in reality, bop singing is just a modern form of so-called "scat" singing. Much as the true bopper will detest the use of the word, only the syllables are new. Where the scat singer used "beeden boden baden" or "lary-a-pa-do," or other unusual sounds, the bopper also has his "ee ee, oo oo, and aa aa," and you'll never find him making use of the other two vowels. "Ee, oo, and ah," are most important to him, but don't wait around to hear "ii" or "oh" in any of his vocal choruses. And don't ask why, cause nobody knows. Of course along with his syllables the singer makes use of the latest in bop melody, harmony, and rhythm, but that is only to be expected.

So there really isn't too much of a mystery about the whole thing. Arrangers are beginning to write it down, which means that the idiom is harnessed if it can be transferred to paper and studied. And there goes the mystery. Familiarity does wonders for bop listeners, and even the commercial radio bands are beginning to sneak bits of it past their sponsors and reach the ears of a public to whom bop has previously been a word as diabolic as "jazz" once was. The stream of music as a whole will go flowing on down through the years, and bop is simply a tributary up which a few venturesome souls wandered first as explorers and pioneers. Eventually it will all be absorbed into what we call *music*, but meanwhile don't fight it—enjoy it. A beret and a beard aren't necessary, and you don't even have to confine your adjectives to "cool" and "crazy." Bop is here to stay and we might as well welcome it as a new and most interesting contribution to the great art of music.

Editor's Notes

PAUL WESTON AND JO STAFFORD began formal work on an autobiography sometime in either early or mid 1979. They assembled their thoughts in outlines and sketches and then proceeded to write their story focusing primarily on the early years of their professional careers. To assist in editing they sought help from Fred Heider, a family friend and former professional colleague. In the late 1940s Fred worked as a script writer for *The Chesterfield Supper Club*, a show that starred both Paul and Jo. It is inferred from correspondence that Fred helped to assemble the rough draft of the autobiography and helped in the preparation of the book proposal.

The book's rough draft and proposal were sent to at least one publisher (Simon and Schuster) in late 1979. After receiving a rejection letter Paul Weston turned to help from the literary agent Rodney Pelter. Both Rodney and Paul worked on getting the manuscript, as it was first prepared, to additional publishers for review. According to correspondence, comments were not flattering towards the proposed book. In a letter to Rodney, dated January 14, 1980, Paul mentioned one publisher critique that stated, "These things happened a long time ago and nobody really cares about them."

The book also suffered from a number of editorial failings, which were alluded to by Paul in a letter to Rodney dated March 17, 1980. He mentioned that the book was a "lost cause" in its present form and that the several criticisms he heard were "valid." One criticism mentioned by Paul in correspondence was that the book did not contain a proper amount of salacious anecdotes. According to Paul, he and Jo would rather keep "telling stories at parties" than write a book of that nature. The planned outline of the book (included in the appendix) does suggest that it was to be filled with anecdotes. However, these anecdotes don't appear, at least from the view of this editor, to be scandalous.

The manuscript was not free from challenges in how it would ultimately be prepared for this printing. For instance, the rough draft was inconsistent in its narrative. Some aspects of the text read as if they were written by a sole author, while others read as if they were done in a tag team style. These parts needed further editing in order to clarify the voice of the authors and to remove any sense of an awkward back-and-forth movement between the writers. For example, the original manuscript used italics as a means of identifying Jo Stafford's voice. This not only looked unusual, but it also created significant problems when identifying things like proper nouns. Great care was taken to not alter the intent of the writers at any time during the book.

Another hurdle was that the manuscript was not fully prepared into one document. Some parts were edited and typed, while others were typed or handwritten without being edited. These writings had to be compiled and then ordered into a narrative that best fit Paul and Jo's story. Only one section had to be left out of the final edit and this related to the couple's love of baseball—as told by Paul. Since this section was incomplete and did not add to the flow of the book's narrative it is included as an appendix.

The most visible change made to the book is perhaps in the title itself. The initial working title was *The Ducks are Drowning*, which is a heading for one of the chapters in the book. It was deemed through a reading of the text and the incomplete nature of the book that the title *Song of the Open Road* was not only more relevant to the content, but also better suited the authors' intent. This editor also believes that the obscure working title contributed to the lack of interest in the original manuscript.

One unfortunate result of the book's premature end in 1980 is that the authors did not have a chance to finish writing their thoughts on paper. What survives is not only an incomplete telling of their autobiography, but also one that is partially slanted. It is unlikely that this was the intent of the authors, as the book's outline does suggest a more balanced approach (see the appendix). The result is a book that represents more of Paul's voice over that of his wife. Fortunately, a series of letters survived that were initiated by Jo Stafford following the early courtship of the couple. These letters not only provide a more balanced view of the couple's relationship, but also add to the time period covered by the autobiography.

The correspondence comprises a period of time from between March and September of 1945. Although some additional letters survive from Jo Stafford following this period, these are the only letters that share a dialogue between Paul and Jo. During the editing process considerable care was taken to ensure that the letters were both readable and faithful to the intent of the writers. Reference notes are included throughout the letters to help aid the reader in understanding context as well as to give background information on some of the people and places that were mentioned.

The editing process for the letters was a challenge in creating balance between readability and the historic nature of the texts. For instance, in many cases spelling and punctuation had to be corrected. A good example of the misuse of punctuation throughout the letters was in the overuse of the comma and em dash. With these errors the former could be changed in some instances to a period and the latter to a comma or parentheses. The reader will also note that italics are used throughout the correspondence. Italics are of course not possible with a typewriter nor are they practical in handwritten correspondence. In some cases, though, Paul or Jo actually underlined words to add emphasis. For consistency, these underlined words were changed to italics. Additionally, if a sentence had a proper noun or a confusing use of speech, italics were added. All of these changes were done when appropriate and did not interfere with the original syntax. If necessary, a bracketed subject was included to correct any random incomplete sentences. Overall, the writing of the authors was quite good considering the informal nature of the letters.

Also included in this publication is a series of essays written by Paul Weston in 1948 and 1949 while he was still a part of the early executive and founding creative team at Capitol Records. These essays provide insight into the philosophy that guided the development of product at Capitol Records throughout the post-war years. They also show that Paul Weston played an important role in shaping the diverse and talented artist roster that came to represent Capitol Records in the years before the industry and cultural shifts of the 1960s.

The first of these writings was an essay that was delivered as an inter-office memo to the top executives at Capitol on December 20, 1948. It was originally untitled and was directed toward Capitol's management in preparation of their launch into classical music with Capitol's acquisition of the German label, Telefunken Records. The acquisition was not only an important step for Capitol in gaining respect and legitimacy in the market, but it also preceded a peculiar legal dispute involving the company's use of the Telefunken catalog.

According to court documents filed in 1949, John Hammond brokered a deal between Keynote Records and Gramophone Works in 1947 to release recordings from the Telefunken catalog. The right to these recordings, as argued in court by Mercury Records (parent company of Keynote Records), went to the Czech government, which owned Gramophone Works and had seized ownership of the recordings as part of a series of war reparations. Capitol, which had started a relationship with Telefunken in 1946, made a separate deal in 1948 directly with the German firm. Capitol claimed in response that the German company had full right to their recordings. Ultimately a judge sided with Capitol Records and declared that they had sole right to release Telefunken recordings since a deal was made directly with Telefunken and was done in accordance with New York copyright law.

The second essay is titled "The Hit Psychology" and was written July 30, 1949, as a response to industry trends that were dominating an increasingly competitive record market. It is inferred through the context of the essay and surviving business records that Paul directed the writing towards Capitol's regional branch managers: William Hill (New York), Vic Blanchard (Atlanta), Paul Featherstone (San Francisco), and Ray Marchbanks (Chicago). At the time, Paul's duties as Capitol's music director led him to be involved in monthly meetings with these regional managers.

The last of Paul's essays is a treatise on bebop published in the May 13, 1949, issue of the British music newspaper, *Musical Express*. Titled "What *Is* Bop?," the writing sheds light on the musical phenomenon of bebop, which in 1949, was being exploited by Capitol Records and other American labels.

The appendixes consist of a number of supporting documents for the autobiography and correspondence. In support of the autobiography are documents that include an unfinished chapter on baseball and the couple's notes for the outline of the book. Complementing the letters are two relevant items. First is a formal and less-than-candid exchange between Johnny Mercer and Jo Stafford in July 1945. These letters were published by Capitol and used as a means of marketing Jo's records and image to the press and dealers. Last is an article (as well as accompanying images) reprinted from the July 1945 issue of *Band Leaders* magazine. The article provides a publicist's view (specifically that of George B. Evans) of Jo's career during the time of the start of her solo career.

KEITH PAWLAK

Keith Pawlak teaches jazz history and is the curator for the jazz and popular music archive at the University of Arizona's School of Music. The archive houses multiple American music collections in addition to the Paul Weston and Jo Stafford Collection. The collections include the libraries of Nelson Riddle, Les Baxter, Artie Shaw, and Linda Ronstadt.

Acknowledgements

THIS BOOK WOULD NOT have been possible without the help of Tim and Amy Weston. Their trust and dedication have opened up a new window to the past. My heartfelt thanks goes to them and to the support of the late Jo Stafford in establishing the Paul Weston and Jo Stafford Collection at the University of Arizona.

I also give thanks to some of the many others who helped make the book and/or collection possible: Bill Marx, Ben Ohmart, Chet Dowling, John Wilson (of the John Wilson Orchestra UK), Rex Woods, Peter McAllister, Sarah Volk, Mia Schnaible, and Mark Heimback-Nielsen. I am also grateful to my colleague Brian Moon for his help in reading the manuscript, as well as to Annette Lloyd, Patricia Hanson, and John Teehan.

Appendices

Ballplayers
and Players

PAUL

The first time I heard the expression "the players," Jack Ryan, the string bass player with the Dorsey Brothers Orchestra, applied it to musicians. Jack joined my recording and radio orchestra in the early forties. His great sense of humor, love for the game of golf, and fine musicianship were part of Jo's and my life for many years.

My experiences with ballplayers began much earlier. As captain and catcher of the Dawes School Midgets in Pittsfield, Massachusetts I came into contact with America's pastime early in life. As a fan of the Eastern League in Pittsfield I watched Lou Gehrig play first base for Hartford, Gabby Hartnett catch for Worcester, and Leo Durocher play shortstop for Springfield.[154] At many a Hollywood party in later years Leo bitterly denied my having seen him the last year before he left for the Yankees and big league play, but I know how old I am and how old he is.

When I joined the Tommy Dorsey Orchestra as an arranger in 1935 I first came to appreciate the life together of "the players" as it related to ballplayers. We both traveled by bus, we both were almost an exclusively male organization (Jo, please forgive me), and we all were really gypsies. "The players" usually played one night in the same town, the ballplayers three days, but the rest was the same. First of all, if you couldn't laugh you couldn't survive. Practical jokes, inside humor, and a relationship completely free of the outside world was part of life on the road. Discomfort was par for the course, but we sure had a lot of fun.

When I left Tommy to come West with Bob Crosby in 1940 I met a completely new group: Eddie Miller, Matty [Matlock], Yank [Lawson], [Bob] Haggart. They were completely consistent with the group I had left and also with the baseball team I had adopted in the Brooklyn Dodgers. When Jackie Robinson was your first real experience with "civil rights" you weren't likely to forget it.

When Jo and Perry Como were the stars for *The Chesterfield Supper Club* in the late forties, I got to meet Frankie Frisch and sit in the booth with him when he broadcast the Dodger games. He was a ballplayer first and a broadcaster a distant second. If a guy hit a triple down the first base line his first three comments would be "Oh boy, oh boy. What a hit!" The radio listener would have no idea where the ball was until the runner was on third.

During those years I developed an attitude as a Yankee hater that was seriously going to endanger my marriage. When Jo and I were married in 1952 she had already developed a love for the Yankees that was to me quite sickening. My diatribes on "buying pennants" and "Yankee luck" immediately put us into a no-win baseball relationship, but we shared a love for the ballplayers, as well as a love for "the players." That compelled us into taking the train to the World Series every year. Several airline escapes had driven Jo to cross-country train travel. So every year we'd work out our schedule so that in October we'd be in New York where it always seemed to [rain.][155]

Chapter Outline

TELEVISION—LIVE!

Al Jarvis—Southern lady's song—"I Hate Those Coons"
Rocket to stardom—Lenny Bruce's fake epileptic fit

Jo Stafford TV—1954
    First show—The silent singer
    Lullaby of Broadway—Going down a stairless subway

Paul Weston—Chevy Shows
    New Year's Eve with Nellie Bly—The Camel pees
    The back timer
    The night they invented champagne
    Crescendo TV's first spectacular—P.W. musical director (stories involving)

        Louis Armstrong, Benny Goodman, Peggy Lee, Rex Harrison, Stubby Kaye, Julie Andrews, Diahann Carroll, Mahalia Jackson, Dinah Washington, Eddy Arnold, Lizzie Miles, and producer Paul Gregory. Benny attacking the control booth, Rex and Louis, Rex and Paul.

ABC—New York—The Stable—Rain on the Roof
    Art Carney, Peter and the Wolf with Ogden Nash
    Joan Sutherland cadenza—a soprano rebels
    Robert Merrill—"You're black, get in the back!"
    Jo's costume change and Lon Chaney's make-up man
    Milton Cross—my name is ????
    Glenn Osser—Wilfred Pelletier's headset

Paul Weston—NY TV
    Sid Caesar writers—Woody Allen, Mel Brooks, Larry Gilbert
    Daily Variety—hot to get robbed
    Larry Gelbart—the Susskind affair
    Ethel Merman vs. Polly Bergen on the Chevy Show

Paul Weston—Danny Kaye Show (four years)
    George Bye—the horse apple story
    Mr. Ito—Revenge for Pearl Harbor
    The Judy Garland show across the hall
    "Get better or get off"
    Acting with Harvey Korman
    Danny makes P.W. downbeat silent
    The barber shop quartet

RADIO—LIVE

Tommy Dorsey—Limehouse Blues
    Amateur swing contest—Bing, Dick Powell, Jack Benny, Ken Murray, Shirley Ross

Paul Whiteman—Dinah Shore and the Friday Night Fights

Duffy's Tavern—Archie vs. Abe Lincoln (*not* the president)

Milton Berle and Charles Laughton—Impossible duo

Paul Weston Show—CBS
    St. Joseph's Cemetery—Music to be Embalmed By

Christmas Sing with Bing—Seven years (Mercer "Glow-worm" lyrics)

Mercer Chesterfield Supper Club—our first show together

Jo Stafford Chesterfield Show
    Mayor of Long Beach
    The missing trumpet player
    Jo and Paul argue coast to coast
    Chesterfields for money, Camels for free

Chapter Outline | 181

The Stafford Sisters
    Bye Bye Blues
    Commercial payoff

BIG BANDS II

Tommy Dorsey—The best of bands
Bunny Berigan—Birdies with booze in the golf bag
Bud Freeman—Feigning and fainting his way from Tommy Dorsey to Benny Goodman. Then Benny Goodman whistles as Bud plays.
The light fingered trumpet player—shoes and razors, etc.
Roy Harris' Symphony—Braille would have helped
Willie the Lion and Fats (come get your lesson)
Texas with Phil Harris—hooker overturns our car

THE BOB CROSBY BAND

My Catalina roommates—Pot fills the air
Lyman Vunk—Letting a high F fly
The sax player and the milkman—Don't screw *my* wife in *my* car on *my* route
The clarinet player and the car horn—beeping and boffing
Real silk—Don't take me 'til I've taken your order

Jimmy Dorsey—Bumblebee Madness

Horace Heidt and Fazola—Booze at the Paramount

Glenn Miller—T.D. payments and Chesterfield
    Arrangements and Schillinger

MORE TOMMY DORSEY

Lew Wasserman as nursemaid
Paul's Phi Beta Kappa Key

The Bernardsville Compound
Oil Wells and the music magazine
Enlisting in the Navy
Sterling Boze in the snow
Marie—the stolen arrangement and the story of *who*
Sleepy Lagoon—*everybody's* fired

THE SINGERS

Stories involving singing stars Paul has recorded with and Jo has sung with.

P.W.—Dinah Shore—Made her first records for Bluebird in late 1930s—three year association as arranger.

Doris Day—Made albums and single records with her for Columbia. Produced the session where she very reluctantly recorded her big hit "Que Sera, Sera."

Ella Fitzgerald—Made 24-song Irving Berlin album with her.

Rosemary Clooney—Recorded with her and also husband José Ferrer.

Betty Hutton—Arranged and conducted her big hits on Capitol—very emotional sessions!

Margaret Whiting—The story of "It Might As Well Be Spring"

Records with Judy Garland, Sarah Vaughan

TV with Kate Smith, Ethel Merman, Marilyn Horne, Helen Traubel, Mary Costa

J.S.—Frank Sinatra—"The most consummate solo singer I ever heard."

Dick Haymes—Few people were aware of what a fine musician Dick was—with a great voice.

Gordon MacRae—We had a million seller together in "Whispering Hope," and many other hit duets.

Frankie Laine—A series of hit duets together in the 1950s—always a joy to work with.

Johnny Mercer—Gave me my first start as a soloist—Taught me to sing rhythm songs.

Nelson Eddy—A true professional—a great to record with.

Bing Crosby—"Sure he was easy going—he could afford to be—always arrived ahead of schedule and always knew his part."

Perry Como—Another "easy goer" who always knew what he was doing—we were Chesterfield salesmen together for years.

Tony Martin—A fine solo singer with very little interest in singing duets. On the Carnation Show I had to lip read to find out where he was going next.

Cowboy duets with Gene Autry and Roy Rogers

THE SONGWRITERS

Personal experiences with some very creative and very colorful characters.

Irving Berlin—*Holiday Inn* was no holiday

Sammy Cahn—Give me "Five Minutes More"—I'll write you another song. But lots of talent!

Jerome Kern—"Young man—here's some advice for you"—while working on *Cover Girl* at Columbia

Richard Rodgers—Sing it like I wrote it!

Johnny Mercer—The all-round lyrical champ

Harry Warren—He loves (?) everybody—"In World War II they bombed the wrong Berlin!"

Johnny Burke—His home was our castle.

Henry Nemo—Why don't they film his life story?

Dave Clark—His office was a fire hydrant outside Lindy's.

The New Yorker—Hollywood adventures of a man who should never have left The Big Apple.

Records

Tommy Dorsey at RCA

Dinah Shore at Bluebird

Bing and Fred at Decca

Lee Wiley at Liberty

The Beginning of Capitol Records

Mercer—Strip Polka
Recording on Wax/Chinese assts/ "Dream" ending
Glenn Wallichs—A distributor in Pittsburg ??
J. B. Conkling—Alan Livingston—To Each His Own
MacGregor Studios
J.S. and P.W. albums

P.W. start of Mood Music—Coronet article
J.S.—Metronome—"A cold singer"
   "Timtayshun"—Cinderella G. Stump
   First folk music album with orchestra.
   Whispering Hope

Columbia Records

The Mannie Sachs adventure.
Paul Weston's triple play—Capitol to RCA to CBS.
Singing Liberace and Luboff—Goddard Lieberson at Carnegie Hall
Bruno Walter and George London
Stravinsky in the control booth.

The Grammy Awards—The Record Academy

Paul Weston as founder and first National President.

Our Own Wide World of Sports

The World Series—"We had to go by train because Jo wouldn't fly at that time. She was a Yankee fan. I was a Dodger fan and the arguments were long, loud and many. There was a constant threat we'd have to come home on separate trains."

The evening with Leo Durocher, Billy Martin, and Mickey Mantle.

Leo's advice bombs on the playing field.

Mickey and Billy become guitar players (?).

Training with the Giants in Phoenix (Dascoli as actor)

Conversations with George Allen—Fiddle players vs. football players

Playing golf with Charles Goren—what a *bridge* player

P.W. in right field at the Coliseum on the Hollywood All Star Team (my kids missed me completely)

In Praise of Excellence

    Singers Unlimited
    Oscar Peterson
    Paul Desmond (Ted Nash)
    Al Burt Carols
    Dave Grusin
    Dick Cathcart
    Doc Severinsen

Today's Music — Jazz returns (via fusion)

Broadway vs. the Rest of Us

Vatican II

    Music in the Church
    Guitar Masses in Beverly Hills
    Paulist Sign of Peace (Lady cries "Bullshit!")
    Jo belted at the altar
    Assorted priest stories

Correspondence
Jo Stafford and Johnny Mercer

July 5, 1945
Dear Prez:

    This is the first time I've had a chance to write, but honestly Johnny, things have been happening so fast that I hope you will forgive me.

    I might as well start by telling you that I've never been happier in my life and certainly I've reason enough to feel that way. Of course, I'll never stop being grateful for all the encouraging things you've done. I guess we all need a helping hand and the generous one you've given me has had much to do with what little success I've enjoyed.

    The six weeks personal appearance at the New York Paramount was one of the pleasantest things I've ever done. I was a fortunate gal to be playing the theatre with a swell picture like *Salty O'Rourke* and to share the stage billing with Charlie Spivak's great band and Dean Murphy.

    Bob Weitman dropped into my dressing room with a contract calling for a return to the Paramount at a figure that nearly floored me. You probably also know that I've just been signed for the permanent spot on the *Ford Hour* on Sundays and I've been doing a bagful of guest radio appearances.

    Johnny, I guess I'm just lucky. I've been doing very well, but really I'm a little bit amazed by it all because honestly, I can't help feeling that luck has a lot to do with it. I've just been fortunate that I've had such wonderful friends like yourself, Paul Weston, Glenn Wallichs, Tommy Dorsey, and Frank Sinatra to give me so much help and encouragement. [Also,] Mike Nidorf, who as an agent is probably the answer to a performer's dream, to handle my business. The gang at G.A.C. have sure kept things jumping for me. I guess you don't need much talent to do okay with that kind of support.

Best to you Johnny, and tell everybody at the office I miss them.

Affectionately,
Jo

Capitol Records, Inc.
Sunset and Vine
Hollywood 28, CA
Phone: Hempstead 3148

July 12, 1945
Dear Jo:

Thanks for your swell note. I don't know what I would rather have happen to me the first thing in the morning, than to find a letter from you. Especially one that at long last grudgingly concedes that you think you're doing fairly well—even if you do excuse it by pointing out that you have just been lucky.

No Jo it's not luck—it's great talent! Knowing you as I do, I can forgive your modesty, but honestly Jo, you've just got to make up your mind that you can attribute it to more than just luck.

I've been looking over your sales figures for Capitol Records and baby, it takes talent (and plenty of it) to do that kind of job. Your record sales are making history. Juke box operators, record shops, disc jockeys, etc. are all shouting your praises and yelling for more of your records. It seems that millions of people know how great you really are—except of course, yourself.

The "*Billboard* Poll" as well as every other popularity poll proved that G.I.'s and young people of the nation are voting you their tremendous favorite. The G.I.'s throughout the world have claimed you for their own. You're tops with them and that's wonderful—"G.I. Jo." You're well on your way and nothing can stop you, not even your own modesty.

I think I can indulge in a little enthusiasm on my own hook because this is one time it's a pleasure to say "I told you so." Here at Capitol we are mighty proud of you and know we will be for a long time to come.

As always, your number one fan,
Johnny Mercer

Singing Star Stafford
by Jehanne Warrington

WHEN JO STAFFORD MADE HER nightclub debut a couple of months ago at Manhattan's swank La Martinique, she was scared to death. Oh, she knew her numbers all right, she had rehearsed like mad, she had a beautiful new gown—everything was set. But Jo was as frightened as if she had never faced an audience before.

Though she had successfully made the jumps from quartet to solo singer to radio to records, this nightclub business was all new to Jo.

"When I heard the introduction to my first song," she says, "I thought, 'Well, here I go—this is probably the end of the Stafford career.'"

On the contrary, it turned out to be the start of a brand new career for Jo. She was a sensation, and the blasé New Yorkers loved her.

To get Jo to leave Hollywood and come East, it took the combined persuasion of her agents, her family, her friends, and practically everybody she knew. They all told her that she should definitely go to New York; she should sing in clubs and theatres and let people who had been buying her records get a look at her. But Jo didn't want to leave home. She was happy in Hollywood, doing radio work and recording and, besides, she didn't think she was right for a nightclub.

"Most of the girls I've seen at clubs are the petite cute little girls who sing with lots of motions and gestures. I'm just not that type. I've always sung without gestures because I thought I looked awkward making them."

"Then, too, I'd always worked right with a band, and the idea of standing out in the middle of a floor alone was simply terrifying. But, I was finally convinced that it was best for my career, so the Martinique engagement was arranged, and off to New York I went, with my fingers tightly crossed."

Paul Weston, musical director for Capitol Records, came East for Jo's opening and made all her arrangements. Besides being one of her best friends, he is one of her greatest fans.

Source: Jehanne Warrington, "Singing Star Stafford," *Band Leaders*, July 1945.

Jo seems to be lost in another world, but she's just intently rehearsing for her debut as a club canary.[156]

"Paul gave me so much moral support that he almost had me thinking I wasn't scared. He kept telling me that it was no different than singing on the air—that I wasn't going to suddenly lose my voice just because I was surrounded by tables instead of microphones. And he kept reminding me of the lyrics of one of the songs I was going to do, 'Ac-Cen-Tchu-Ate the Positive.' Whatever psychology he used on me, it must have worked, because after the first few bars of my opening number, I wasn't so frightened, and somehow or other, everything turned out okay."

"After I got into the routine of it, I really loved nightclub work. It was fun and exciting. And I got a big kick out of dressing up in evening gowns every night. But I haven't deserted radio. Right now I'm only doing guest appearances, but I hope to have my own program one of these days."

Jo is one of those rarities, a native Californian. Though born in Coalinga, she considers Long Beach her home, because her family moved there when she was four-years-old. She made her first public appearance when she was eleven, singing in a trio, with her elder sisters, Pauline and Christine. She attended Long Beach Polytechnic High School and majored in music. After her graduation, the Stafford Sisters sang on many radio programs in Los Angeles. When her sisters married, Jo joined a group of seven boys who called themselves The Pied Pipers. The group was later reduced to The Pied Pipers quartet. In 1938, when Tommy Dorsey came to Los Angeles on one of his tours, he heard them and signed them for his band.

One day during rehearsal, Jo was singing a new number by herself when Tommy happened to walk in. He had never heard Jo alone before, and he was so impressed with her ability that he decided right then and there that she should sing solos too. That was the beginning of a long association with Dorsey, during which time Jo sang with the quartet and was featured as a soloist on many of Tommy's biggest record hits.

Frank Sinatra joined Dorsey about two months after Jo, and they are still close friends.

Jo says that the experience she had travelling around the country with the Dorsey band was invaluable and helped to pave the way for her later appearances on radio and records.

"After four years with the band, I was tired of one-nighters and busses and trains, so The Pied Pipers and I came back to California and went into radio. Then, when Johnny Mercer did his first program for Pepsodent, the Pipers and I went on the show and I sang ballads besides singing with the boys."

About this time Mercer and Buddy De Sylva formed the Capitol Records company and Jo was one of the first singers they contracted. She made recordings both as a soloist and with the Pipers. Jo remained with the boys until she was signed for the *Chesterfield Music Shop Program*.[158] The show was to be five times weekly, and she realized that she couldn't sing with the group and do her solos as well, because it involved too much rehearsal time. So she got her friend June Hutton to take her place with the Pipers.

When the program went off the air, Jo had many offers for other air shows. But her agents and Johnny Mercer felt she should go to New York.

The "Champion" and "Josie" when Frank attended Jo's nightclub opening.[159]

So she finally decided to accept the Martinique offer and now, after her tremendous click, she isn't sorry. She does confess, however, that she gets homesick once in a while.

"I guess I'm just a home girl," she says, "because I don't like living in hotels. And I do miss my family. But my sister, Christine, is with me, so it isn't too bad. And anyway, I know that to be a success in the music world you've got to do some traveling. I learned that when I was with the band."

Johnny Mercer is supposed to have said, in speaking of the Stafford pipes, "That girl picks pockets with her voice." And the way they wear her records out in juke boxes, we can see what he meant.

Yes, Miss Jo does all right for herself with that smooth voice of hers.

Bibliography

ASCAP Biographical Dictionary. New Providence, N.J.: R.R. Bowker, 1980.

Bach, Bob, and Ginger Mercer. *Our Huckleberry Friend: The Life, Times and Lyrics of Johnny Mercer.* New York: Citadel Press, 1982.

Dexter, Dave, Jr. *Playback.* New York: Billboard Publications, 1996.

Giddins, Gary. *Bing Crosby: A Pocketful of Dreams—The Early Years, 1903-1940.* New York: Little, Brown and Company, 2001.

Jablonski, Edward. *Harold Arlen: Rhythm, Rainbows and Blues.* Boston: Northeastern University Press, 1996.

Kinkle, Roger. *The Complete Encyclopedia of Popular Music and Jazz, 1900-1950.* Westport, CT.: Arlington House, 1974.

Lees, Gene. *Singers and the Song.* New York: Oxford University Press, 1987.

Marshall, Jim. *Jo Stafford.* Last modified August 2008. http://web.cfa.arizona.edu/westonstafford/JoDiscography.pdf

Simon, George. *The Big Bands.* New York: Collier, 1974.

The Paul Weston and Jo Stafford Collection. http://web.cfa.arizona.edu/westonstafford/.

Notes

1. Glenn Wallichs was the owner and operator of Music City, a highly influential and trend-setting record store, which opened on the Northwest corner of Sunset and Vine in Hollywood in 1940. Glenn, Buddy De Sylva, and Johnny Mercer founded Capitol Records in 1942.
2. *Johnny Mercer's Music Shop* was the result (premiered on June 22, 1943). The show also marked the moment that Paul changed his birth name Wetstein to his stage name, Weston.
3. This is a reference to the 1948 AFM recording ban.
4. Flit is the brand name for an insecticide that has since been discontinued.
5. This album was retitled and released by Corinthian Records in 1982 under the name *Darlene Remembers Duke, Jonathan Plays Fats*.
6. Date inferred from the content of the letter.
7. Paul Weston.
8. Dario Goldfarb and Jim Vernon were operators of the La Martinique nightclub, which was located in the basement of 57 W 57 St. Goldfarb owned the establishment, whereas Vernon was presumably his business partner. Jo Stafford opened at the La Martinique on February 8 and was originally featured during the midnight segment of the floor show. The orchestra was led by vocalist and bandleader Carl Ravazza and showcased Jo in the following songs (in order): "Saturday Night," "I Promise You," "Ac-Cen-Tchu-Ate the Positive," "I Didn't Know," "Candy," and "Embraceable You."
9. Prez refers to Johnny Mercer. He was President of Capitol Records from February 1944-September 7, 1947.
10. John Hud refers to John Huddleston. He was a former member of The Pied Pipers and was married to Jo Stafford from 1941-1943.
11. Natch is southern slang for naturally or of course.

12. The War Manpower Commission was tasked by the War Productions Board in early 1945 to further efforts already enacted by the government to conserve low coal stockpiles. From February 26, 1945-May 8, 1945, all businesses providing entertainment were required to close at midnight or force a penalty. Among the affected businesses were nightclubs, bars, and sporting events. The curfew would have forced the La Martinique to shorten its floor show.
13. "I Promise You" was recorded by Jo Stafford in Los Angeles with Paul Weston and His Orchestra on October 4, 1944.
14. "Merc" refers to Johnny Mercer.
15. Ella Mae Morse was Capitol Records' first artist discovery, which was a result of her 1942 hit recording of "Cow Cow Boogie."
16. The Sicilian roots of Louis Prima fueled the prejudices of many people during the time to lump him in a category with Negro entertainers. Jo Stafford is likely referencing this prejudice in a lighthearted manner.
17. John refers to Johnny Mercer. Pish and tosh is an expression that politely interjects condescension towards a subject. It normally appears as pish tosh, not pish and tosh.
18. Christine and Pauline were Jo Stafford's sisters.
19. Oh well.
20. Postmark date.
21. Mike Nidorf was Jo Stafford's personal manager.
22. Ken Dolan was a high profile celebrity agent in the 1930s and 1940s. He was also married to the actress and singer Shirley Ross.
23. President Franklin D. Roosevelt passed away on April 12, 1945.
24. Mildred was likely an assistant to Jo Stafford.
25. Bing refers to Bing Crosby.
26. Postmark date.
27. Ted Steele led the Ted Steele Orchestra, which provided music for the *Chesterfield Supper Club* from January-September 1945.
28. *Hobby Lobby* was a popular CBS radio show. A Clark Bar was a crunchy peanut butter candy bar covered in milk chocolate. Gil Johnson was a ballet dancer featured in the La Martinique floor show.
29. "A Friend of Yours" was recorded April 2, 1945, at Capitol's Los Angeles studio. "On the Sunny Side of the Street" and "Conversation While Dancing" were recorded September 13, 1944, in Los Angeles.
30. Gordon refers to Gordon Jenkins.
31. Auto-Lite refers to the CBS *Auto-Lite Radio Show* featuring Gordon Jenkins and His Orchestra.
32. Katherine Cornell was a highly celebrated actress of the American stage.
33. Foster "Ruck" Rucker (a.k.a. Galen Drake). He was married to Pauline

Stafford and was also a well-known personality on radio. His radio show, *This Is Galen Drake*, aired from 1945-1958. *For Whom the Bell Tolls* was recorded in 1943 by Victor Young and His Orchestra for Decca Records.

34. Chris refers to Christine Stafford. Christine was not only Jo Stafford's sister, but also worked as her personal secretary.
35. Reference to "I Promise You."
36. Paulish means in the style of Paul Weston.
37. "I Should Care" was written in 1944 by Paul Weston, Axel Stordahl, and Sammy Cahn.
38. Mary Ashworth preceded Jo Stafford as vocalist on the *Chesterfield Supper Club*.
39. Tom Rockwell formed the General Artists Corporation and was a business colleague of Mike Nidorf.
40. George B. Evans was the publicist for Frank Sinatra and Jo Stafford at this time.
41. Walter Winchell was a syndicated newspaper columnist popularly known for his gossip on celebrities and politicians.
42. Emily Post was an author popular for her books on etiquette.
43. *Harvey* was a Broadway play produced at the 48th St. Theatre that ran from November 1, 1944-January 15, 1949.
44. *The Late George Apley* was a Broadway play produced at the Lyceum Theatre that ran from November 23, 1944-November 17, 1945.
45. Frank Fay played Elwood P. Down in the Broadway production of *Harvey*.
46. The Adams refers to the Adams Theatre in Newark, NJ.
47. Paul Weston was Margaret Whiting's music director during this time at Capitol Records. Paul had dated Margaret Whiting for a short period of time and the relationship was likely over by this time.
48. George T. Simon was editor-in-chief of *Metronome* magazine from 1939-1955.
49. Home refers to the Stafford family home in Long Beach, California.
50. Annie O'Grady was Paul Weston's Mother.
51. Postmark date.
52. "Stop, Look and Listen" was recorded December 14, 1937.
53. The Tropics was a popular Polynesian restaurant in Beverly Hills at the time. It was opened by Harry "Sugie" Sugarman in 1936 and lasted until 1953 when it was renamed The Luau. The restaurant was a regular hangout for people in the motion picture industry.
54. Vivian Della Chiesa was a popular lyric soprano star on radio during the 1940s and 1950s.
55. This was Lois Butler's recording debut as a 14-year old soprano. She re-

corded "Italian Street Song," "Romany Life," and "When You're Away" with Paul Weston and His Orchestra on April 20, 1945.
56. Jim refers to James B. Conkling. He was a classmate of Paul Weston's at Dartmouth College. He was hired, at the urging of Paul Weston, to be the head of Capitol's recording activities.
57. Reference to the NBC *Ford Show*.
58. Charlie Wick was a booking agent at the William Morris Agency.
59. 1944 popular song written by Hugh Martin and Ralph Blane. Paul Weston later arranged the song for inclusion on Jo Stafford's first album, *Songs by Jo Stafford*. They recorded the song in Los Angeles on October 31, 1945.
60. George "Bullets" Durgom, celebrity agent.
61. Jimmy Walker was mayor of New York from 1926-1932. Walker was a Roman Catholic with Irish roots.
62. Margerie "Tootsie" Crawford's young son. "Tootsie" was Jo Stafford's niece and the daughter of Jo's sister Christine.
63. "Flintheart" refers to the 1935 motion picture *Private Worlds*
64. Postmark date.
65. Father Charles Edward Coughlin, Roman Catholic priest who wielded considerable power during the 1930s through a network radio program.
66. B.O. palace refers to body odor palace. She is presumably referring to the beginning of her six-week engagement at the Paramount Theatre as the opening headliner for the film *Salty O'Rourke*. Backing Jo was the band leader and trumpet player Charlie Spivak. Also appearing was the comedian Dean Murphy and the Charlie Spivak band vocalists Jimmy Saunders and Irene Daye.
67. Reference to an April 27, 1945, recording date with Jerry Colonna and The Pied Pipers performing "Bell Bottom Trousers" and "Kashmiri Love Song." The latter song went unissued by Capitol Records.
68. *Your Hit Parade* was a popular radio series on CBS that focused on the popularity of individual songs and not on the popularity of artists.
69. Reference to Johnny Mercer's "Dream," which had only been on the Billboard charts for a little over a month.
70. Larry Brooks was a radio singer and actor.
71. CBS radio show sponsored by Borden Milk and formally known as *The Ginny Simms Show*.
72. An April 25th review of her Paramount Theatre appearance by Billboard reviewer Bill Smith was critical of her lack of up-tempo numbers. According to the review, Jo opened the show with "I'm Beginning to See the Light" and closed with "I Didn't Know About You."
73. Norman Foley was the head of the publishing firm M. Witmark & Sons

during this time.
74. Postmark date.
75. Scottish form of Elizabeth, meaning 'chosen by God' or 'consecrated by God.'
76. The Stanley Steamer automobile. It had a steam-powered engine and was made from 1902-1924.
77. Dick Todd was a Canadian singer who was popular on American radio during the 1930s and 1940s.
78. Margaret Whiting was a Capitol Records artist at the time of the letter.
79. Johnnie Johnston recorded "Wait and See" on July 2, 1945.
80. The previous paragraph ended with a dry ink pen.
81. Axel Stordahl.
82. Musicraft Records built a reputation in the 1930s and 1940s by undercutting the major record labels with budget priced records distributed through drug and chain stores.
83. Dave Dexter, Jr. Dexter was the editor of Capitol's newsletter, the Capitol News, and was also a talent scout for the label. His activities were primarily focused on developing the label's jazz artists.
84. This is a sly reference to two popular songs. The first song, "That's Why Darkies Were Born," was written by Ray Henderson and Lew Brown for the 1931 edition of George White's Scandals. The song was both a social satire and celebration of the history of the American Negro. The second song, "The Birth of the Blues," was written by Ray Henderson, Buddy De Sylva, and Lew Brown for the 1926 edition of George White's Scandals.
85. Another sly reference to a popular song. "I'm Glad There Is You" was written in 1941 by Jimmy Dorsey and Paul Madeira.
86. G.A.C. is an abbreviation for the General Artists Corporation.
87. Postmark date.
88. Dave Dexter, Jr. was also an outspoken music critic. This is a reference to Dexter's criticism of the popular bandleader Al Donahue.
89. Bing Crosby's first wife was an actress and dancer named Wilma Winifred Wyatt, who went by the stage name Dixie.
90. Reference to Paramount Picture's 1946 release of Irving Berlin's *Blue Skies*.
91. "Moss" refers to the booking agent Harry Moss. He was head of the Harry Moss Agency and a vice president of the Willard Alexander agency.
92. This is a reference to a session made by Stan Kenton in Chicago on May 4, 1945, in which he recorded "Tampico" and "Southern Scandal."
93. This is meant as a joke.

94. Glenn Wallich's wife was Dorothy Kueker. They were married on September 27, 1933, and had two children: Linda and Susan.
95. Mickey Goldsen was the CEO of Criterion Music, a subsidiary of Capitol Songs, Inc.
96. Reference to CBS Radio's *Your Hit Parade*.
97. Postmark date.
98. This is presumably a reference to Rudolph Valentino. He was an Italian actor and sex symbol of the 1920s.
99. In other words—where will fate take me this week?
100. Shirl-girl refers to Shirley Mitchell. Paul Weston and Shirley Mitchell were dating at the time.
101. New York trumpet player and orchestra leader. He was signed to a contract with Decca Records in 1945.
102. Toots Shor's Restaurant was located at 51 W 51st St. in Manhattan. The proprietor, Bernard "Toots" Shor, befriended many of the celebrities of the time period. Jules Stein was the founder of the Music Corporation of America.
103. Buddy De Sylva, songwriter and founder of Capitol Records.
104. St. Patrick's Cathedral.
105. Postmark date.
106. Cold in my head.
107. Lowery refers to Chuck Lowery of The Pied Pipers.
108. Norman Blackburn was a talent scout, producer, and program director (most notably with NBC). Carroll Carroll was a writer for television and radio shows.
109. Renaldo may refer to the song "Renaldo," which was performed by Carl Ravazza at the La Martinique.
110. Postmark date.
111. Leave you know is slang for I will let you know.
112. For the week ending May 31, 1945, "Candy" was the most-played jukebox record.
113. Jill Warren was a female disc jockey and entertainment columnist for the magazines *Movieland* and *Band Leaders*.
114. *Pagliacci* was an Italian opera written by Ruggero Leoncavallo in 1892.
115. Reference to the 1935 motion picture *Private Worlds*.
116. Broadway play that ran at the Morosco Theatre from 1943-1947. The film adaptation featuring Ronald Reagan and Eleanor Parker premiered in 1948.
117. Sy Oliver was an arranger for Tommy Dorsey.
118. This session, which was led by Billy Butterfield and His Orchestra, went unissued by Capitol Records. The following songs were recorded:

"Gee, It's Good to Hold You," "The Wish That I Wish Tonight," "As Long As I Know You're Somewhere," and "The Last Time I Saw You."

119. Popular CBS radio show of the time formally known as the *Texaco Star Theater*.
120. Jo Stafford recorded "Gee, It's Good to Hold You" and "That's for Me" with Billy Butterfield and His Orchestra on July 2, 1945. The previous recording of "Gee, It's Good to Hold You," made on June 20, 1945, went unreleased.
121. Johnnie Johnston was in the Billboard record charts at this time with a Capitol Records release of "Laura." It was recorded March 6, 1945, with Paul Baron and His Orchestra. Johnnie recorded "Wait and See" and "Autumn Serenade" with Carl Kress and His Orchestra on the same New York recording date with Jo Stafford.
122. Criterion Music (Mickey Goldsen) published "Gee, It's Good to Hold You." "That's for Me" is the song they are referring to from *State Fair*.
123. Railway route that ran from Chicago to Los Angeles. The Chief was part of the Atchison, Topeka and Santa Fe Railway.
124. Dave Dexter, Jr., Christine Stafford, and Mickey Goldsen.
125. Tom Martin was a booking agent at General Artists Corporation.
126. Polly Adler was a New York madam who ran a popular brothel and clubhouse during the 1920s that catered to politicians, gangsters, and celebrities. She was retired and living in Los Angeles in 1945.
127. Sam Steifel took over personal management of Andy Russell during George Durgom's time in the service. After Durgom's discharge Sam Steifel turned over all management responsibilities except those involving finance. Durgom also took over personal management of The Pied Pipers at this time.
128. Date inferred from the content of the letter.
129. Frank Sinatra's personal manager.
130. Reference to June Hutton. June replaced Jo Stafford in The Pied Pipers singing group.
131. George Walter Mercer was Johnny Mercer's brother.
132. Harold refers to Harold Arlen.
133. Frank Merriwell was a popular fictional character created by Gilbert Patten under the pseudonym Burt L. Standish. The character existed in some form on books, radio, and comic strips from 1896-1949.
134. Frank Sinatra recorded "Day by Day" with Axel Stordahl and His Orchestra on August 22, 1945.
135. Reference to the Borden family murders of August 4, 1892.
136. Short lived Broadway musical that ran from July 18, 1945-December 8, 1945.
137. Slang for brought down.

138. 1941 popular song written by Allie Wrubel and Charles Newman. Jo Stafford loosely paraphrases from the original lyrics.
139. *Stella Dallas* was a popular soap opera on radio that lasted from 1937-1955 and was based on a 1923 novel by Olive Higgins Prouty.
140. Postmark date.
141. Bonnie was Jo Stafford's cousin.
142. Hughie Prince was a producer for Jo's September engagement at the La Martinique. He also wrote the 1941 hit, "Boogie Woogie Bugle Boy."
143. Dr. Sigmund Spaeth, otherwise known as the "The Tune Detective," was a celebrity musicologist who was featured on radio, newspapers, and television from the 1930s-1950s.
144. La Martinique nightclub.
145. The La Martinique had scheduled floor shows at 8:30pm, 12:30am and 2:30am. Jo Stafford is presumably referring to the midnight show, not the 2:30am show.
146. It isn't clear if this song title refers to the 1934 Harry Warren and Al Dubin song, "I Only Have Eyes For You."
147. "On the Atchison, Topeka and the Santa Fe."
148. Accomplished actor of Broadway and vaudeville during the 1920s.
149. Gibson Holler is an area near Gainesboro, Tennessee.
150. This presumably refers to the cowboy singer Billy Wilson, who was popular during the 1940s.
151. Both Mike Nidorf and George Durgom maintained a long friendship with the Weston household.
152. Reference to Martin Block's *Make Believe Ballroom* radio show. Jo Stafford won best female vocalist in the poll that aired on February 3, 1945. In that poll she beat Dinah Shore by 13,000 votes.
153. Paul Weston, "What *Is* Bop?," *Musical Express*, May 13, 1949.
154. Gabby Hartnett played for the Worcester Boosters during the season of 1921. Leo Durocher played during part of the 1925 season before being signed to the New York Yankees. Lou Gehrig played for the Hartford Senators during the seasons of 1921, 1923, and 1924.
155. This last word was penciled out and was partially illegible.
156. Original caption. Photograph by Edward Ozern. From the office of George B. Evans. Photograph courtesy of the Paul Weston and Jo Stafford Collection at the University of Arizona School of Music.
157. Jehanne Warrington, "Singing Star Stafford," *Band Leaders*, July 1945, 26-27.
158. *Johnny Mercer's Music Shop*
159. Original caption. Photograph by Edward Ozern. From the office of George B. Evans. Photograph courtesy of the Paul Weston and Jo Stafford Collection at the University of Arizona School of Music.

Index

"A Friend of Yours," 92
"Ac-Cen-Tchu-Ate the Positive," 67, 115, 190
"Again," 161
Alexander's Ragtime Band (film), 12-13
"Almost Like Being in Love," 80
"Alone Together," 124
"Am I Blue," 95
Anything Goes (musical), 7
Arlen, Harold, 134
Arus, George, 40-41
Ashworth, Mary, 94
Astaire, Fred, 9, 63, 65
Avakian, George, 72, 73

"Baby It's Cold Outside," 162
"Baby Won't You Please Come Home," 95
Barron, Blue, 160-61
Bauer, Joe, 37
Beiderbecke, Bix, 38
Bennett, Robert Russell, 103, 110, 112, 120, 127, 131
Berlin, Irving, 59, 63, 108, 182, 183, 184
Bing Crosby Kraft Show, The (radio program), 13
Blackburn, Norm, 114
Block, Martin, 142, *151*
"Blue Moon," 95
"Boy Next Door, The," 98-99, *100*, 131

Brooks, Larry, 103, 114, 115, 118, 124, 137, *149*
Brooks, Randy, 112-13, 114
Burnett, Carol, 74
Burns, Bobby, 27-29
Bushkin, Joe, 40-41
Butterfield, Billy, 66, 95, 122, 128
"Buttons and Bows," 160

Cahn, Sammy, 59, 126, 138, 183
California Melodies (radio program), 12
Captain from Castile, The (book), 140, 142
"Candy," 67, 89, 102
Cantor, Eddie, 97, 99
Capitol Theatre, 49
Carousel (musical), 118, 120
Carroll, Carroll, 114
Chesterfield Supper Club, The (radio program), 12, 67-68, 91, 94, 127, 132, 137, 138, 141, 169, 178, 180, 181, 183, 191
Christy, June, 23
Clark, Dave, 59-60, 184
Clock, The (film), 115
Cole, Nat "King," 23, 24, *29*, 66-67, 133
Colonna, Jerry, 100, 102, 105
Como, Perry, 91, 92, 94, 132, 160-61, 162, 178, 183
Conkling, Jim, *53*, 67, 68, 97, 103, 107, 108, 116, 155

"Conversation While Dancing," 92, 115
Copa, The, 88
Copland, Aaron, 157
Cornell, Katherine, 92
Cover Girl (film), 63, 183
"Cow Cow Boogie," 66
Crosby, Bob, 9, 25, 63, 65, 66, 178, 181
Crosby, Bing, 9, 13, 25-26, 35, 47, 65, 90, 108, 160, 183
"Cruisin' Down the River," 160, 161

D'Amico, Hank, 95
Daley, Casss, 108
Dark of the Moon (play), 118
Davis, Joan, 7, 126, 131
"Day by Day," 134, 138
Dear Ruth (play), 118
Decca Records, 9, 112-13, 160-63, 184
De Sylva, Buddy, 66, 68, 100, 108, 113, 191
Dexter, Dave, 67, 105, 108, 125, 127, 128
Dick Haymes Show, The (radio program), 97
Dolan, Ken, 90, 114, 134
Dorsey Brothers Orchestra, The, 6, 35, 177
Dorsey, Jimmy, 35
Dorsey, Tommy, 6, 8, 9, 13-15, 21-22, 25, 28, 35-52, 60-61, *84*, 177, 180, 181, 184, 187, 191
Drake, Galen (see Foster "Ruck" Rucker)
"Dream," 67-68, *82*, 105, 109, 131, 134, 184
Durgom, George "Bullets," 99, 109, 130, 134, 138, 139, 142

Elman, Ziggy, 45, 128, 132
"Embraceable You," 94
Enchanted Cottage, The (film), 116-17
Evans, George, 94, 172

"Far Away Places," 160, 161, 162
Fatool, Nick, 73
Faye, Alice, 7, 12-13

Feather, Leonard, 101, 126
Ferretti, Andy, 8
Fibber McGee and Molly (radio program), 120
Fleischman Hour (radio program), 7-9
For Whom the Bell Tolls (film), 92, 96
Freeman, Bud, 8, 181
Freeman, Ticker, 62

"Galway Bay," 160-61
Garry Moore Show, The (TV program), 74-75
Gastel, Carlos, 23-25
"Gee, It's Good to Hold You," 119, 122, 127
General Artists Corporation, 106, 129, 187
Gillespie, Dizzy, 166
Gillette, Lee, 68-69, 94
Glass Menagerie, The (play), 118
Goldfarb, Dario, 87, 88, 129
Goldkette, Jean, 38
Goldsen, Mickey, 109, 122, 127, 128
Goodman, Benny, 22, 25, 179, 181
Grammy Awards, 77, 185

Haggart, Bob, 119, 178
Hamilton, Joe, 74
Handley, Alan, 79-81
Hannan, Walter, 109
Harris, Roy, 155-57
Harvey (play), 95, 120, 123
Haymes, Joe, 6-9, 35
Herman, Woody, 128, 132
Hit Parade (radio program), 102, 105, 162
Hokinson, Helen, 74
Holiday Inn (movie), 9, 63, 65, 183
Holtz, Lou, 140
Hope, Bob, 67
Hopper, Hedda, 133
Huddleston, John, 45, 88, 99, 136

Hutton, Betty, 123, 125, 132, 182
Hutton, June, 67, 133, 191

"I Promise You," 88, 90, 94, 103
"I Should Care," 94, 97, 101, 105, 109
"I'm Beginning to See the Light," 112
"I'm Comin' Virginia," 95
Irwin, Ginny, 13

Jack Benny Show, The (TV program), 75-76
James, Harry, 48
Jarvis, Al, 101, 105, 108, 109, 125, 127, 179
Jenkins, Gordon, 92, 97, 161
Johnson, Gil, 91
Jones, Spike, 160

Kearney, Joe, 25-26
Kelly, Gene, 63
Kemp, Hal, 12
Kenton, Stan, 23, 67, 109, *113*
Kern, Jerome, 63, 183
KHJ (radio station), 11-12
King, Alyce, 13
King, Donna, 67
King Sisters, The, 13
King, Vonnie, 13
King, Wayne, 122
Knight, Evelyn, 160, 161, 162
Kress, Carl, 95
Kueker, Dorothy, 109
Kyser, Kay, 160

La Martinique, 103, 129-30, 133, 138, 140, 141, *144-146*, 189, 192
Lane, Ken, 62, 126
Late George Apley, The (play), 95
Laura (film), 117
"Laura," viii, 109, 118, 120
Lee, Peggy, 23, *30*, 67, 179

Leiss, Oscar, 114
Leonard, Jack, 13, 47
Levy, Al, 133
Lewis, J.C. Jr., 12
Lindy's (restaurant), 59, 184
"Little Bird," 160, 161
"Lonesome Road," 95
Lowery, Chuck, 114
"Long Way Home," 90
Luboff, Norman, 77, 185
Lyman, Abe, 125

MacRae, Gordon, 160, 162, 183
"Mañana," 160, 161, 162
Marinka (musical), 136
Martin, Jeannie, 71
Martin, Tom, 129
Matlock, Matty, 66, 178
May, Billy, 21
McGarity, Lou, 95
Mercer, Johnny, 65-68, *82*, *83*, 88, 103, 108-109, 110, 114, 116, 117, 119, 122, 125, 127, 130, 133-34, 137, 139-42, 162, 180, 183, 184, 187-88, 191-92
Merman, Ethel, 12, 180, 182
Miller, Eddie, 66, 178
Mitchell, Paul, 6-7, 9
Mitchell, Shirley, 112, *113*
Mondello, Toots, 8
Monroe, Vaughn, 161
"Moonlight in Vermont," 66
Moore, Garry, 74-75   Morgan, Russ, 160-61, 162
Morse, Ella Mae, 66, 67, 88, 90, 109, 115, 125, 132
Moss, Harry, 109
Murray, Arthur, 128
Music for Dreaming (album), 66
Music Maids, The, 13

Musicraft Records, 105, 114
"My Darling," 160, 162

"Nature Boy," 160, 161-62
Nidorf, Mike, 90-92, 94, 97, 103, 105, 108, 111-18, 126, 128-30, 132, 134-38, 141-42, *150*, 187

O'Brien, Margaret, 125, 139
O'Day, Anita, 132
Oliver, Sy, 119
"On the Atchison, Topeka and the Santa Fe," 140
"On the Sunny Side of the Street," 92, 115, 140
"Out of This World," 101, 124
Owens, Harry, 115, 125

Palmer House, 47
Palomar Ballroom, 13
Paramount Theatre, 29, 49, 90, 94, 101, 103, *104*, 106, 109, 114, 115, 118, *147*, *149-50*, 181, 187
Parsons, Louella, 90
Petrillo, James, 68, 162, 163
Pied Pipers, The, 13-15, 44-45, 47, 49, *55*, 66, 67, 73-74, 131, 191
Philco Show (radio program), 88
Prima, Louis, 89
Prince, Hughie, 140

Raye, Don, 138
Remick Music (music publisher), 61-62
Rich, Buddy, 40
"Riders in the Sky," 161
Ritter, Tex, 109, 125
Rockwell, Tom, 94, 117, 118, 137
Roosevelt, Franklin, 90, 92
Roseland Ballroom, 6, 8
Ross, Shirley, 92, 180
Rucker, Foster "Ruck," *17*, 92, 99, 131
Russell, Andy, 114, 125, 130-31, 138

Sanford, Herb, 13-14
Sauter, Eddie, 119
Shapiro-Bernstein (music publisher), 61
Shelley, Dave, 66-67
Shore, Dinah, 48, 62, 90, 92, 108, 160, 180, 182, 184
Silvers, Phil, 65
Simon, George, 21-22, 48, 95, 107
Sinatra, Frank, viii, 40-41, 44, 47-48, 133-34, 138, *146*, *150*, 182, 187, 191, *192*
Sillaway, Ward, 8
Slack, Freddie, 66
"Slow Boat to China," 160
"Some Enchanted Evening," 161
Song of Norway (operetta), 118, 124
Stafford, Bette, 106, 110
Stafford, Bonnie, 138
Stafford, Christine, 11-12, 89, 92, 95, 105, 109, 110, 114, 117, 126, 128, 131, 138, 141, 191, 192
Stafford, Pauline, 11-12, *17*, 89, 92, 95, 99, 107, 110, 131, 141, 191
Stafford Sisters, The, 11-12, 181, 191
Star Spangled Rhythm (film), 65
State Fair (film), 119-20, 122
Steele, Ted, 91, 94
Steiffel, Sam, 114
Stein, Jules, 113, 115
Stoloff, Morris, 63
Stone, Cliffie, 68
"Stop, Look and Listen," 97
Stordahl, Axel, 13-14, 23-24, 29, *53*, 60-61, 105, 126, 128, 133, 138
"Strip Polka," 65, 184
Stulce, Freddie, 49

Taps, Jonie, 61
Telefunken Records, 155-57
"That's for Me," 119-20
"There's No You," 97, 101

Tilton, Martha, 109, 114, 115
Toscanini, Arturo, 92, 96, 101, 104
Tough, Davie, 42-43
Townsend, Irving, 72
Travis, Merle, 68-69
"Tree in the Meadow," 160, 162
"Twelfth Street Rag," 160, 162

Ulanov, Barry, 126
Up in Central Park (musical), 118

Vallée, Rudy, 7-9, 131
Van Heusen, Jimmy, 61-62, 65
Van Steeden, Peter, 126
Vernon, Jim, 87
Victor Records, 95, 155-57, 161-63
Voice of the Turtle, The (play), 119

"Wait and See," 105, 116, 120
Wallichs, Glenn, 66-67, 69, 105, 108, 109, 113, 115, 116, 122, 125, 138, 155, 184, 187

Warren, Bobby, 120
Warren, Harry, 59, 61, 184
Warren, Jill, 118, *150*
Welles, Orson, 190
Weston, Tim, 76
Wettling, George, 95
Whiting, Margaret, 66, 95, 105, 160, 161, 162, 182
Whitmark Music (music publisher), 62
Whittinghill, Dick, 73-74
Wick, Charlie, 98, 107, 115, 136
William Morris Agency, 114
Williams, Roger, 73
Wilson, Billy, 141
Winchell, Walter, 94, 97, 99
Wynn, Ed, 75-76
Wynn, Nan, 62

"Yah Ta Ta," 120
"Yesterdays," 124
Young, Victor, 9, 92

www.ingramcontent.com/pod-product-compliance
Lightning Source LLC
Chambersburg PA
CBHW070740160426
43192CB00009B/1508